MW00567155

Supersensible Knowledge

Supersensible Knowledge

Rudolf Steiner

Anthroposophic Press
Hudson, New York

Rudolf Steiner Press
London

The thirteen lectures presented here were given between October 1906 and April 1907 in Berlin and Cologne. In the collected edition of Rudolf Steiner's works, the volume containing the German texts is entitled, *Die Erkenntnis des Übersinnlichen in unserer Zeit und deren Bedeutung für das heutige Leben*. (Vol. 55 in the Bibliographic Survey.) They were translated from the German by Rita Stebbing.

Published in the United States by the Anthroposophic Press, Bell's Pond, Star Route, Hudson, NY 12534.

Published in the United Kingdom by Rudolf Steiner Press, 38 Museum St., London WC1.

Library of Congress Cataloging-in-Publication Data
Steiner, Rudolf, 1861-1925.
Supersensible knowledge.

Translation of: Die Erkenntnis des Übersinnlichen in unserer Zeit und deren Bedeutung für das heutige Leben (vol. 55 in the Bibliographic survey).
Thirteen lectures presented between October 1906 and April 1907 in Berlin and Cologne.
1. Anthroposophy. I. Title.
BP595.S894E7513 1987   299'.935   87-17520
ISBN   0-88010-190-3   cloth Anthroposophic Press
ISBN   0-88010-191-1 paper
        85440-255-1 cloth Rudolf Steiner Press
        85440-265-9 paper

Cover: Graphic form by Gerard Wagner

Printed in the United States of America

Contents

Lecture I

The Significance of Supersensible Knowledge Today

Berlin, October 11, 1906

This lecture is meant as an introduction. The aim is to acquaint the audience with the kind of issues investigated by spiritual science, for example, our relation to the spiritual world, evolution and destination, the riddle of birth and death, the origin of life and that of evil, health and illness, and problems of education. During the winter lectures, the scope of spiritual investigation will become apparent. These lectures will also deal—from a spiritual-scientific viewpoint—with subjects such as burning social problems and the tasks facing modern humans. The discourses will demonstrate that spiritual science is not a mere theory, but an inherent necessity in present-day life.

Although a great variety of age groups are represented in the audience, the subjects to be discussed should contain something of interest for everyone. Each lecture will be self-contained, yet also have a connection with the rest. The title of the next lecture, "Blood is a very special fluid," may sound rather sensational, but it is in fact a subject that points to significant aspects of humanity's evolution, on which only spiritual science can throw light. Later lectures will deal with subjects such as, "Man's Existence in the Light of Spiritual Science"; "Who are the Rosicrucians?"; "Richard Wagner and Mysticism"; "What Do Educated People Know About Theosophy?"; and a lecture about religion, "The Bible and Wisdom."

Those in the audience who attended lectures last winter will hear about things that are familiar, though presented from a different aspect. The results of spiritual-scientific investigation can only be fully understood when illumined from different sides. As I said, today's lecture is to serve as an introduction to this winter's programme that will demonstrate what is meant by spiritual-scientific investigation, and the significance of such research of the supersensible for humanity now and in the future.

The Theosophical movement emerged thirty years ago,* and soon spread world wide. Yet, after thirty years of intensive work, it has not the best reputation. Many people regard Theosophy as something fantastic with no relation to facts, something that belongs in a cloud-cuckoo-land. It cannot be denied that it has often been badly presented, usually through overeagerness and lack of knowledge; at times perhaps even charlatans helped to undermine its reputation. However, today we are concerned with the significance Theosophy can have in the lives of individuals.

The prejudices that exist against Theosophy are strong and widespread. Some regard it on a par with spiritism, as something irreconcilable with modern science. People who are engaged in scientific pursuits, or those that simply feel that solution to significant questions can be found in modern science, see no point

*The Theosophical Society was founded in 1895.

2

in devoting themselves to something which seems to contradict well-documented scientific discoveries. They regard Theosophy as illogical, and its appeal restricted to dreamers.

Another kind of prejudice comes from religious quarters. There are people who, because of their calling, feel they must protect religion from Theosophy, or they fear that if they accept it, it will create conflict with their religious conscience. They assume that Theosophy aims to establish a new religion or sect.

Yet another kind of prejudice stems from the mistaken view that Theosophy is a revival of ancient Buddhism. Here the fear is that in place of Christianity the world is to be inoculated with a kind of neo-Buddhism. Nothing that one can say appears to dispel these three kinds of prejudice.

If Theosophy aimed to transplant an ancient religious system into Europe, it would sin against its own fundamental principle, which is to understand every religion and spiritual aspiration. Every great philosophy or world outlook has arisen out of the configuration of a specific civilization; it is not possible to transplant it into a completely different culture. If modern human beings, standing within the European-American civilization, are to receive the impulse for true spiritual progress, it must spring from the vigorous life of their own time. Such impulses cannot be derived from views and ideas of a bygone age; they must have their roots where the human soul has its home. What is needed is the recognition that the inherent possibility in our own culture must be widened and deepened. While every civilization has within it fully matured abilities and inclinations, it also contains seeds for its further evolution. If these seeds are allowed to lie fallow, they become burning questions weighing on the human soul.

The seeds for future development in the hidden recesses or a person's inner being must evolve out of necessity.

There is no conflict between the world outlook of spiritual science and the great religions. Spiritual science, while resting on its own foundation, seeks to understand all religions. It wishes to show that all the great world religions are based on the same fundamental truth. From these lectures it will become apparent that spiritual science reflects an aspect of all of them. Far from wanting to become another religion, spiritual science aims to awaken understanding for the views of the past as well as for those which, because they are right for the present time, will truly further mankind's progress in the future.

Let us objectively consider why spiritual science would neither wish to be a religion nor found a new sect. The lectures to be held this winter will increasingly demonstrate that the time is past for founding new religions. Spiritual truths can no longer be presented the way they were in former times. Founding new religions came to an end with the central religion, Christianity. Christianity is capable of endless development far into the future. Spiritual science should be a means to make Christianity more accessible to the scholarly mind. Its foremost task is to contribute to the comprehension of religion by illumining the wisdom it contains, and by enabling people to find their way into spiritual life. There is no need for new religions; the old ones contain all the wisdom and knowledge we require. What *is* needed is to present that wisdom in a new form. In so doing, the old forms will also become understandable. The true value of the ancient religions will be restored by spiritual science.

Greater tolerance in regard to religious views has come about in recent times. Modern human beings feel that to hate and persecute those who confess a different faith serves no purpose. In fact, the hatred and intolerance that formerly caused so much blood to flow in the name of religion is no longer understood. This tendency to accept and tolerate will continue for a time, but eventually it will prove too weak, too insipid an attitude for progress. When in the nineteenth century the transition took place to a more tolerant attitude, it was a blessing. At that time it was justified and it helped to develop love and humanness. However, what is right and good in one age is not necessarily so in another. The various epochs of world evolution provide human beings with different tasks. The feeling and attitude that was fully justified in the nineteenth century, which kindled noble hopes in human hearts, will prove too feeble and ineffective in the twentieth century when other soul forces are called upon.

What is required now is complete mutual understanding, not just tolerance and patience. So far, Christians have tended to take the attitude that, while they do not understand the faith of Muslims or of the Jewish people, and equally they do not understand Christianity, each one tolerates the other's views. This attitude will prove insufficient. In the future, complete understanding is necessary. Human beings must be able to recognize that their faith has developed within a certain culture and that it determines their thoughts and ideals. But life is shared with people of different cultures and with different views, and these a person must endeavor to understand. The truth should result in more than mere patience and tolerance; it should enable a person to enter with understanding into what the others feel and experience. A person's comprehension of Truth must encompass all other faiths.

This is an attitude that is very different from that of

mere tolerance. Through spiritual science a person should be able to progress to complete understanding. The followers of particular faiths must realize that they have reached certain aspects of Truth, and that Truth takes on different forms in different souls. This is to be expected and should be no cause for division; rather Truth in all its forms should act as a unifying force. Such an attitude is positive and humane, and brings people together. Also, it is on a higher level than tolerance, and has a greater ennobling effect on the human soul because it is based on insight and love.

Helena Petrowna Blavatsky[1], founder, always saw Theosophy as having the mission to provide knowledge. She recognized that modern human beings are always bound to ask (a) questions concerning a person's fate and destination, birth and death, infinity and eternity; (b) questions about illness and pain; and (c) about what happens after death when a person has laid aside the body. Every human being asks these questions. The task of religion has always been to provide spiritual rather than merely theoretical answers, to give a person strength, consolation and reassurance.

From religion, we are meant to obtain answers to the crucial questions of existence. Religion should enable us to go through life fulfilling daily tasks, feeling calm and secure, and possessing knowledge that reaches beyond everyday affairs to encompass immortality. If we understand the human soul, then we know that no one can be strong and capable unless a certain comprehension of the riddles of life are reached. Only knowledge prevents them weighing on the soul, giving rise to doubt and uncertainty that makes a person weak. Without inner security of knowledge, a person is lost when faced with greater issues and unable to cope even with everyday affairs.

It will increasingly be recognized that insightful knowledge is the only true basis for vitality and strength of soul. The theosophical movement acknowledges this fact and sees it as its task to provide such knowledge. But why the need for spiritual science when through all the epochs of evolution, religion has existed to answer life's burning questions? The answer is that times have changed. What satisfied our ancestors no longer satisfies modern people. There is plenty of evidence of that today, and it will become even more obvious as time goes on. Religion does of course answer many questions, but the answers are formulated in a way that leaves people dissatisfied. The reason is that human nature has changed, and this leads people to attempt to find substitutes for the answers that no longer satisfy them either in history or in natural science.

People who longingly seek answers in modern science are especially those to whom the Bible and religion no longer speak. But modern science has to acknowledge that it has no answers to life's most important questions. Its enormous achievements in the realm of physical data are fully acknowledged by spiritual science; the results arrived at through painstaking research spanning the whole globe are indeed impressive. But when it comes to questions about the meaning of life or mankind's future evolution, it fails to provide answers. Those who have tried, and the many who are still trying, to find through natural scientific investigation what religion no longer provides, discover only disappointment. By contrast, spiritual science exists for the very purpose of throwing light on life's riddles and burning questions. However, those who still find satisfaction in what traditional religion has to offer will be unable to recognize what spiritual science is about, but what satisfies one today may not do so tomorrow. The founder of the Theosophical Society saw it as an ideal to provide concrete knowledge about life's deepest riddles. The claim that spiritual research is scientific is fully justified, as anyone will acknowledge who becomes acquainted with the methods whereby it is carried out. It aims to provide a spiritual world view with a scientific basis that will speak to the most erudite and also the simplest mind.

Yet there are those who feel that Theosophy is an interference and that it is better to leave people with their old faith, or better still to do something to restore the old faith, as science is incapable of providing answers to spiritual questions. That is an unrealistic view; people who hold it do not see what is happening all around them. Theosophy endeavors to be fully conscious of the tendencies that are coming to the fore. Let one example suffice to illustrate the urgent necessity for a world outlook based on spiritual insight.

Let us consider for a moment what is taking place in a country where for centuries religion has had a strange history. In Spain, orthodox religious faith has up till now had a strong grip on its people. But a change is taking place in this country where religious influence extends even to trivial everyday affairs. Who would have thought, a few years ago, that what we are now witnessing could possible occur in Spain. Only a short time ago the ruling power would have nothing to do with any so-called modern ideas. Just consider how rigid was the faith of the woman who preceded her son, the present king, Alphonso XIII. She has had no inclination to deviate one iota from the ways and customs that over the centuries have become firmly entrenched in the whole fabric of the state. Imagine the contrast to what is taking place now: This woman sits in Lourdes where she can indulge in the old ways and customs, while in Spain the young king is obliged to allow new ideas to saturate the rigid system. A liberal minister is shaking up the establishment, and is ruthlessly introducing new laws on education and marriage.

This is a sign that the impulses of the time (*Zeitströmungen*) are making themselves felt, and against that, mere human opinion is powerless. What must come about is proper understanding of the change in attitude that is taking place. Most of those in office are blind to such changes. They are unprepared and do not know what to do. It is not realized that neither such impulses are stronger than arbitrary opinions, nor that the needs of humanity at a particular time must be met with understanding and open minds. In our time people are too conscious to just accept what is imposed upon them. But everyone is required to understand the impulses of the times in which we live, and guide these impulses in the right direction. In no other way can healthy progress be ensured. History is made by human beings, but when it is made in spite of them, the result is chaos. Harmony and justice can come about only through cooperation. The age one lives in makes demands; it is up to the individual to recognize what they are. Just to sit-back in comfort and let things take their course is not enough. That is an attitude that rather hampers progress. The impulses of one's age must not be ignored. Human beings are destined to absorb into their heart and mind, into their whole being, impulses from the supersensible realm, so that they become effective in the world.

What does that imply? A thoughtful person will recognize that very much is implied in what has just been said. It is obvious to deeper insight that without a foundation of spiritual life, no material civilization can prosper. No state, no community has ever endured without a religious foundation. Let someone earnestly try to found a community consisting solely of people whose interests are purely materialistic, that is people with no knowledge of spiritual things, who accept as valid only materialistic views. Things would not deteriorate into chaos straightaway only because people would still have a vestige of ideas and ideals. No social system can endure unless it is built upon the foundation of religious wisdom. An individual is a bad practitioner who believes that practical minds are enough to ensure success. A person who wants to see material conditions continue to make progress must recognize that a foundation of spiritual insight and religion is imperative. If we want to give a human being bread, we must also give him something that will nourish the soul. In the periodical *Lucifer*, I once wrote that no one should be given bread without receiving also a world outlook—that to give bread without giving also spiritual sustenance could only do harm. At first sight, this statement may not seem valid, but in the article it is substantiated.

What is taking place in Spain is only a special instance of what is happening everywhere. One must be an ostrich with one's head in the sand not to see it. But what is it that is needed at the present time to further true progress? The need is for specialized knowledge. Just as special knowledge is necessary for the provision and distribution of material necessities like clothing, so is special knowledge necessary for meeting a human's spiritual needs.

Ancient civilizations have depended upon the trust placed in priests and wise men. We must not criticize the systems of past cultures; they have been suitable for their particular epoch. When a culture is no longer acceptable, for the people can no longer live according to the old customs, the remedy does not lie in fighting it, but— in change and progress of the spiritual life. In earlier times people turned to the priest for words of comfort and assurance. Today we need spiritual investigators, people who can speak about the supersensible world in ways that correspond to our time, and are therefore acceptable and understandable to modern humans.

Let us consider what is to be done if things remain the way most of our contemporaries find satisfactory. The situation in Spain can be regarded as symptomatic. Perhaps you think that old arrangements will give way to new ones and people will become accustomed. But no new arrangement will have a chance of success unless there is also a change of heart. A spiritual outlook must begin to pulsate like life-blood through our whole modern civilization. When conflict arises nowadays over spiritual or social issues, there is nowhere people can turn for counsel concerning life's most important questions.

Let us look at what usually happens in such cases. Many people expect to find through natural science, that is, through knowledge of physical data, the kind of answers that have formerly been obtained from religion. Recently a conference of scientists took place in Stuttgart where weighty problems were discussed. (But can it be said that modern human beings are able at such places to find answers to spiritual questions? To questions concerning eternity or the meaning of death? At such conferences it becomes apparent that modern physical research is embarking on some strange investigations.) For those with interest in these things, I may mention that at Stuttgart methods were discussed in detail concerning the way organs from one organic being could be transplanted into another. Another point of great interest was the way the advent of the microscope had transformed all research. Now it was possible, by mixing and dissolving certain substances, to produce from lifeless matter something with the semblance of life. Many more things were mentioned, all of which called for respect and admiration in regard to modern scientific research.

But people wonder about the sense and purpose of all the extraordinary things physical researchers are busy investigating. Who is there among the scientists of this modern Olympus of cultural life that can answer questions about the meaning of life? No attention was given to questions of this nature at the latest scientific conference, whereas only two years ago Ledebur[2], a chemist from Breslau, made an extraordinary speech in which he pleaded for psychological research to be stopped. And it is noteworthy that at a gathering of scientists Theodor Lipps[3] could still speak on the subjects: natural science and philosophy. In the midst of reports on purely physical research, he threw in remarks to the effect that, unless natural science is able to arrive at a spiritual understanding of the phenomenon of man, it will never reach the status of a world view. "When man," he said, "looks into his inner being, he finds the 'I,' and when he widens it to encompass the 'world-I,' he finds contentment."

The situation is truly extraordinary. After all, the theosophical movement, where you will not find such vague general answers given to important questions, has existed for thirty years. Theosophy discusses subjects, such as a person's life before birth and after death, his experiences when attaining spiritual sight and so on, concretely and in detail. But what happens? After such specific knowledge has been available for thirty years, these issues are dealt with in commonplace and trivial ways that cannot possibly satisfy anyone. When the most important questions of life are discussed, all that is offered is a web of unworldly abstract thought—nothing but a play on meaningless words that appeals only to people with an interest in abstract philosophy. When those who long for answers to the heart's deepest questions turn to official authorities, they find nothing but powerlessness and ignorance.

Yet it is of utmost importance that there should exist, within external science, advancing as it does at great speed, a center of spiritual life, a place where human beings can find concrete knowledge about supersensible issues—a knowledge that would throw light also on the spiritual content preserved in old religious faiths and customs. If knowledge of the spiritual world is presented with the same scientific acumen as natural science, it would speak to the human soul and influence social life, just as was formerly the case with religion. Once that happens, religious life will assume new forms, while the old forms that have become influenced by materialism will disappear.

It is very important that the full significance of religion is recognized. Today there are many people—in France it is very much the fashion—who say that morality can be established without religion. It is maintained that humans be moral without religion. This shows no comprehension whatever of spiritual laws. If religious worship is traced through the consecutive historical epochs, it will be found that a new cult arose in each, with special significance for that particular time. The cult of Hermes arose in Egypt, in India, the Rishis, in Persia, Zarathustra, and among the Hebrews emerged the cult of Moses. In our time, it is Christ Jesus, the greatest founder of religion in modern times. These cultures became great because their exponents understood the needs of their time. The exponents of Christianity will also work effectively when once again the needs of the human heart are understood.

When a civilization comes into being, the primary constituent is always religious faith, that is, a sum of views, feelings and ideas about what is regarded as spiritually the most exalted. There will be awareness that the world's foundation is of divine origin, and that death is vanquished. All the great civilizations draw their spiritual creativity from the faith on which they are founded. The great creative works of ancient Egypt, Persia, Greece, and Christian times would never have come into existence had they not originated from human thought and beliefs. Indeed, even the most materialistic culture stems originally from a person's knowledge of the supersensible. Thus, the most basic constituent of a civilization is faith.

The second thing of importance to consider is the effect of this faith on an individual's inner life. The thoughts and ideas a person formulates about supersensible matters have an uplifting effect; they fill a person's soul with feelings of harmony and joy. Whenever people have felt inwardly happy and secure, aware that their lives have a higher meaning, it has always been due to religious faith. Such feelings transform themselves into contentment and confidence in life. Thus, it can be said that when a civilization comes into being, we first of all recognize the presence of faith, and second feelings of exaltation, contentment and confidence in life.

The third thing to consider belongs to the sphere of the will. This is the sphere of morality and ethics. Ethics, that is, moral philosophy, influences not only morals, and acts of will, but also all social arrangements, all laws, and all affairs of state. It influences art, which belongs to the sphere of feeling. To think that morality can exist without religion is an illusion. Morality arises in the sphere of feeling. At first a person will have certain opinions about spiritual issues; second these will give rise to feelings of contentment and security; and third to will impulses that tell him: This is good; that is evil.

How does it come about that so many are subject to the illusion that morality can be established without the foundation of religion? It happens because morality, this third component of a culture, is the last to disappear. When a civilization declines, the first to diminish is faith, that is, doubt arises about religion. However, even if the invigorating certainty of faith is absent for a long time, people still retain the feelings engendered by faith. When at last even inherited religious feelings have vanished, the morality that originated from the faith will still persist. Those who today believe that morality exists without a foundation of religious faith do not themselves have to rely on such an impossibility. They subsist on the remnant of inherited moral qualities. It is only because they have retained the morality of the past that people who think spiritual qualities are mere fantasy can act morally. Many believe they have overcome the need for religion, yet their moral life originated from religion.

Socialists tend to want to establish morality without a foundation, that is, without religion. The reason they can talk about the subject at all, and the reason also for things not collapsing into chaos straightaway, is solely that they retain in the bodily organism the old morality that they want to eradicate. Even the political changes socialists want to bring about are based on the old morality. If progress is to come about, there must be a renewal of spiritual knowledge. When it is possible to draw people's attention to the spiritual forces that are streaming into our world all around us, this knowledge will create feelings of security and impulses towards moral actions in their soul. Then we will no longer have to rely on riches inherited from the past, but on those that spring from our own culture.

There is nothing illogical in the knowledge of higher worlds of which spiritual science speaks. The supersensible is not treated as something remote and inaccessible; it is extraordinary that certain philosophic views maintain that no educated person can believe in a supersensible world. Such views demonstrate ignorance of the specific sense in which spiritual science speaks about the supersensible. I have often made clear by means of the following comparison what I mean by that.

For someone born blind, the world of color and light is a "beyond" in relation to the accessible world. In other words, we have access to a world only if we have organs with which to perceive it. The moment sight is restored an individual no longer has to rely on others in order to determine that light and color exist. Then, a person experiences a new world but one which in reality was always there. In regard to the spiritual world of which spiritual science speaks, the situation is exactly the same.

Knowledge of the spiritual world is again attainable through spiritual science. Just as there always were enlightened human beings able to see into the spiritual world, so there are individuals today who have developed spiritual organs. They are able to perceive the spiritual aspect of physical phenomena and see beyond the portal of death. They perceive that part of the human being constitutes the immortal being that survives after death. Their task is to impart detailed information of this spiritual research, thus making spiritual knowledge possible once more.

It is cheap to say: Give me the means to see for myself. Actually, anyone can attain the means, provided that person seeks guidance of the right kind. Spiritual science constitutes such guidance and it is accessible to everyone. The very first requirement, however, is the ability to rise above the usual way of looking at things. The person must, as it were, say: Here is someone who tells me he can see into the spiritual world, and who relates many specific details. He speaks about what happens to humans after death, about spiritual forces and beings that are invisible to ordinary sight, and that permeate the world about us. As yet I cannot see that world, but if I keep an open mind and pay attention to my feelings and inner sense for Truth, I shall know whether what I hear sounds probable or the reverse. I can further apply logical thinking to the matter, and see if life itself bears out what I am told. Having listened calmly to everything and found nothing to contradict common sense, I shall attempt to look at the world in light of this knowledge and see if it explains human destiny. By assuming spiritual scientific views to be correct, I will be able to test whether they explain things and make life understandable. I shall also gradually discover if spiritual knowledge does give one inner strength, joy and confidence in life. In other words, I will discover whether there is a basis for accepting the words of the initiate. This attitude I adopt is the same in regard to spiritual knowledge as that adopted by a remarkable person in regard to the ordinary world of light and color.

The life of the deaf, mute and blind Helen Keller[4] was often described. Up to the age of seven, she was like a little wild animal. Then there came to her a teacher of genius, Anne Sullivan, and then her education was far above average. She had never heard sound or seen color and light; all her life had been one of silent darkness. But she had allowed everything that those around her experienced of color, light and sound to affect her soul. Recently a new book of hers was published, entitled *Optimism*. This small volume showed that not only was she knowledgeable about the affairs of the present time, but also about the life and language of the Greeks and Romans. Although she had never experienced it herself, she described the beauty of creation conveyed by sight and hearing. Her little book showed that she had gained more than just mental pictures from what had been described to her; she had gained inner strength and confidence in life.

In the same way, people who do not close their mind will gain strength, confidence and hope for the future from listening to the description of someone with spiritual sight and hearing. Inner uncertainty causes weakness, and creates an inability to cope with life. Individuals who listen to someone with spiritual sight will gradually become aware of things that they were not aware of before. Spiritual knowledge will make people efficient and capable. Impulses must flow from the spiritual world like new life-blood and permeate our political and social systems, bringing about a transformation of our whole civilization. You must realize that spiritual knowledge is in our time closely connected with the most important questions and problems. When these press in upon us from all sides in various forms, we must acknowledge the need for deeper understanding. That the spiritual-scientific view of the world is shaped through prophetic knowledge of what must come will be born out by the lectures to be held this winter. They will throw light not only on the great civilizations, but also on everyday life. The results of spiritual research show clearly what is needed to ensure the healthy progress of mankind, and also what provides the individual with inner strength, courage and joy in life.

There are still many who laugh at what spiritual science has to say about supersensible issues. As they believe they are practical folks, they will have nothing to do with such unpractical nonsense. But the spiritual-scientific movement will carry on its work. The time will come when even people who are now among the fainthearted, skeptical doubters will turn to those who have absorbed spiritual knowledge because they need solutions to the great riddles and questions that will burden the soul— not arbitrary human questions, but questions posed by life with great force. Already in the near future, spiritual knowledge will be needed more and more if human evolution is to progress.

Lecture II

Blood is a Very Special Fluid

Berlin, October 25, 1906

The title of today's lecture no doubt reminds you of a passage in Goethe's *Faust*, when Faust, representing striving man, enters into a pact with evil powers, represented by the emissary from hell, Mephistopheles. Faust is to sign the pact in blood. At first he regards this as a joke, but Goethe undoubtedly meant the words spoken by Mephistopheles at this point to be taken seriously: "Blood is a very special fluid."

Goethe[1] commentators usually provide curious interpretations of this passage. You will be aware that so much has been written about Goethe's *Faust* that it can fill libraries. I naturally cannot go into what every commentator has said about this particular passage, but it all amounts more or less to what is said by a recent commentator, Professor Jacob Minor.[2] Like others, he regards Mephistopheles' remark to be ironic, but Minor adds a curious sentence. I quote it in order to illustrate the amazing things said about Goethe's *Faust*. Minor states: "The devil is an enemy of blood." He goes on to point out that as blood invigorates and sustains human life, the devil, being an enemy of the human race, must of necessity be also an enemy of blood. Minor is quite right when he further demonstrates that in sagas and legends blood always plays the kind of role it plays in Goethe's *Faust*. The oldest version of the Faust legend clearly describes how Faust makes a slight cut in his left hand with a penknife, dips a quill in the blood in order to sign the agreement, and as he does so, the blood, flowing from the wound, forms the words: "Oh man, escape!"

This is all quite correct, but what about the remark that the devil is an enemy of blood and for that reason demands the signature written in blood? Can you imagine anyone wishing to possess the very thing he abhors? The only reasonable interpretation of the passage is that Goethe, as well as earlier writers of Faust legends, wishes to show that the devil regards blood as especially valuable, and that to him it is important that the deed is signed in blood rather than in neutral ink. The supposition must be that the representative of the powers of evil believes, or rather is convinced, that he will gain a special power over Faust by possessing at least a drop of his blood. It is quite obvious that Faust must sign in blood, not because the devil is his enemy, but because he wants to have power over him. The reason behind this passage is a strange premonition that if someone gains power over an individual's blood, one gains power over the person. In short, the feeling is that blood is a very special fluid and it is the real issue in the fight for an individual's soul between good and evil.

A radical change must come about in our modern understanding and evaluation of the sagas and myths handed down since ancient times. We cannot go on regarding legends, fables and myths as childlike folklore or pretentiously declare them to be poetical expressions of a nation's soul. The poetic soul of a nation is nothing but a fantasy product of donnish officialdom. Anyone with true insight into the soul of a people knows with certainty that the contents of fables and myths, depicting powerful beings and wonderful happenings, is something very much more profound than mere invention. When with knowledge provided by spiritual research we delve into sagas and myths, allowing the mighty primordial pictures to act on us, we begin to recognize the profound ancient wisdom they reveal.

To begin with, one naturally wonders how it was possible for primitive man, with his unsophisticated views, to depict in the form of fables and myths, cosmic riddles that are unveiled and described in exact terms by means of modern spiritual research. This at first seems very surprising. However, as further research reveals how these ancient fables and myths came into existence, one ceases to be amazed, and all doubt vanishes. One discovers that myths and fables, far from containing naive views, are filled with primordial wisdom. A thorough study of myths and fables yields infinitely more insight than today's intellectual, experimental sciences. Admittedly the approach to such a study must be with spiritual scientific methods. Whatever legends have to say about blood is important, because in earlier times an individual's inherent wisdom made him aware of the true significance of blood, this special fluid that in human beings is a stream of flowing life.

Whence this wisdom came in ancient times is not our concern today; it will be the subject of a later lecture, though an indication will be given at the close of this one. Today we shall look at the significance of blood in human evolution and its role in cultural life. However, our discussion will not be from a physiological, or any other natural scientific point of view, but from that of spiritual science. It will be a help if before pursuing our subject we remind ourselves of a maxim that originated within the civilization of ancient Egypt, where the priestly wisdom of Hermes held sway. This maxim, which expresses a fundamental truth, is known as the Hermetic maxim and runs as follows: As above, so below.

All kinds of trivial explanations of this saying are to be found, but the one that concerns us today is the following. It is obvious to spiritual science that the world accessible to our five senses, far from being complete in itself, is a manifestation of a spiritual world hidden behind it. This hidden world is called, according to the Hermetic axiom, the "world above, or the upper world." The sense world spread all about us, perceptible to our senses and accessible to our intellect, is called the "world below," and is an expression of the spiritual world above it. The physical world is therefore not complete to the spiritual researcher, but is a kind of physiognomic expression of the soul and spirit world behind it, just as when looking at a human face one does not stop short at its shape and features, but recognizes them as an expression of the soul and spirit behind them.

What everyone does instinctively when faced with an ensouled being, the spiritual researcher does in regard to the whole world. The axiom, As above, so below, when applied to a human being, means that a person's soul impulses come to expression on the face. A hard, coarse face demotes coarseness of soul, a smile inner joy, and tears inner suffering.

Let us now apply the Hermetic axiom to the question: What is wisdom? Spiritual science has often pointed to the fact that human wisdom is related to experience, particularly to painful experience. For someone actually in the throes of pain and suffering, the immediate experience will no doubt be inner discord. But when pain and suffering have been conquered, when only their fruits remain, a person will say that from the experience a measure of wisdom is gained. The happiness, enjoyment and contentment life brings one gratefully accepts; but more valuable by far, once it is overcome, is the pain and suffering, for to that people owe what wisdom they possess. Spiritual science recognizes in wisdom something like crystallized pain; pain transformed into its opposite.

It is interesting that modern research, with its more materialistic approach, has come to the same conclusion. A book well worth reading was published recently about the mimicry of thought. The writer is not an anthroposophist, but a natural scientist and psychologist. He sets out to show that a person's thought life reveals itself in the physiognomy, and draws attention to the fact that a thinker's facial expression always suggest assimilated pain.

Thus, you see emerging, interspersed with more materialistic views, a confirmation of an ancient maxim that originated from spiritual knowledge. This will happen more and more frequently; you will find ancient wisdom gradually reappearing within the framework of modern science.

Spiritual research confirms that everything that surrounds us in the world: the configuration of minerals, the covering of vegetation, the world of animals, is the physiognomic expression of the life of spirit behind it. It is the "below" reflecting the "above." Spiritual science maintains that what thus surrounds us can be properly understood only when one has knowledge of the "above," that is, knowledge of the prototypes, the primordial beings from whom it all originated. Today we shall turn our attention to that which creates on earth its physiognomic expression in the blood. Once the spiritual background of blood is understood, it will be recognized that such knowledge must of necessity influence our spiritual and cultural life.

The problems human beings are facing today are momentous and pressing—especially educational problems involving not only the young but also entire populations. These particular problems are bound to increase as time goes on. The great social upheavals taking place make this evident to anyone. Demands causing anxiety are continually made, whether in the guise of the woman question, the labor question or the peace question. These are all problems that become understandable once insight is gained into the spiritual nature of blood.

Another question, similar in nature, which is again coming to the fore, is that of race. The racial problem cannot be understood unless one understands the mysterious effect when blood of different races is mingled. And finally, there is the problem of colonization that also belongs in this category. This problem has become even more pressing since attempts have been made to tackle it more consistently than was formerly the case. It arises when cultivated people are to share their lives with uncultivated people. Certain questions ought to be asked when attempts are made to tackle the problem: To what extent is it possible for a primitive people to assimilate a strange culture? Can a savage become civilized? What here comes under consideration are vital and far-reaching questions of existence, not just concern about doubtful morality. It is unlikely that one will find the right way of introducing a strange culture to a people if it is not known whether it is on an ascending or descending line of evolution; whether this or that aspect of its life is ruled by its blood. When the significance of blood is discussed, all these things come under scrutiny.

The physical composition of blood will be known to you from science in general. In humans, and also in the higher animals, blood is truly the stream of life. Our inner bodily nature is in contact with the external world through the fact that we absorb into the blood the life-giving oxygen from the air, a process by which the blood is renewed. The blood that meets the instreaming oxygen acts as a kind of poison, as a kind of destroyer within the organism. This blue-red blood, by absorbing the oxygen, is transformed into red, life-giving blood through a process of combustion. This red blood that penetrates all parts of the organism has the task to absorb directly into itself substances from the outer world, and deposit them as nourishment along the shortest route within the body. Humans and the higher animals must of necessity first absorb nutritive substances into the blood, then, having formed the blood, absorb into it oxygen from the air and finally build up and sustain the body by means of the blood.

A knowledgeable psychologist once remarked that the blood circulating through the body is not unlike a second person who, in relation to the one made of bone, muscle and nerve, constitutes a kind of outer world. And indeed our entire being constantly takes from the blood what sustains it, and gives back what it cannot use. One could say that a person carries in his or her blood a double (Doppelgänger) who, as a constant companion, furnishes him or her with renewed strength and relieves a person of what is useless. It is entirely justified to refer to blood as a stream of life and compare its importance with that of fibre. What fibre is for the lower organism, blood is for the human being as a whole.

The distinguished scientist Ernst Haeckel[3] has probed deeply into nature's workshop, and in his popular works he quite rightly points out that blood is the last to develop in an organism. When tracing the stages of development in a human embryo, one finds rudiments of bone and muscle long before there is any indication of blood formation. Only late in embryonic development does formation of blood and blood vessels become apparent. This leads natural science to rightly conclude that blood made its appearance only late in world evolution, and that forces already in existence had first to reach a stage of development comparable to that of blood before they could accomplish what was necessary in the human organism. When as embryoes human beings repeat once more the earlier stages of human evolution, they adapt to what existed before blood first made its appearance, This a person must do in order to achieve the crowning glory of evolution: the enhancement and transmutation of all that went before into that special fluid that is blood.

If we are to enter into the mysterious laws of the spiritual realm that hold sway behind blood, we must first take a brief look at some of the basic ideas of spiritual science. You will come to see that these basic ideas are the "above," and that this "above" comes to expression in the laws that govern blood, as it does in all other laws, as if in a physiognomy.

There are in the audience some who are acquainted with the basics of spiritual science; they will allow a brief repetition for the sake of others who are present for the first time. In any case, repetitions help to make these basic ideas clearer, as light will be thrown on them from a different aspect. In fact, what I am going to say may well appear as just a string of words to those who as yet know nothing about spiritual science, and are therefore unfamiliar with this outlook on life. However, when ideas behind words seem to have no meaning, it is not always the ideas that are at fault. In this context a witty remark made by Georg Christoph Lichtenberg[4] is apt. He said: If a head and a book collide and the result is a hollow sound, it is not always the book's fault. So, too, when some of our contemporaries pass judgment on spiritual truths, which to them seem like a string of words, it is not always spiritual science that is at fault. However, those acquainted with spiritual science will know that the references made to higher beings are to beings that really do exist, even if they cannot be found in the physical world.

Spiritual science recognizes that humans, as they appear in the sense world to physical sight, represent only a part of their true being. In fact, behind the physical body there are several more principles that are invisible to ordinary sight. Human beings have the physical body in common with the so-called surrounding lifeless mineral world. In addition, they have a life body, or ether body. What is here understood by ether is not that of which natural science speaks. The life body or ether body is not something speculative or thought out, but is as concretely visible to the spiritual senses of the clairvoyant as are physical colors to physical sight.

The ether body is the principle that calls inorganic matter into life and, in lifting it out of lifelessness, weaves it into the fabric of life. Do not for a moment imagine that the life body is something the spiritual investigator thinks into the lifeless. Natural science attempts to do that by imagining something called the "principle of life" into what is found under the microscope, whereas the spiritual investigator points to a real definite entity. The natural scientist adopts, as it were, the attitude that whatever exists must conform to the faculties a person happens to have; therefore, what he or she cannot perceive does not exist. This is just about as clever as a blind person saying that colors are nothing but a product of fantasy. The person to pass judgment on something must be the one who has experienced it, not someone who knows nothing about it.

Nowadays one talks of "ignorabimus" and "limits of knowledge"; this is possible only as long as human beings remain as they are. But, as spiritual science points out, we are constantly evolving, and once we develop the necessary organs, we will perceive, among other things, the ether body, and will no longer speak of "limits of knowledge." Agnosticism is a grave obstacle to spiritual progress because it insists that, as human beings are as they are, their knowledge can only be limited accordingly. All that can be said to this is that then human beings must change, and when they do they will be able to know things they cannot now know.

Thus, the second member of a person's being is the ether body, which one has in common with the vegetable kingdom.

A human being's third member is the astral body. This name, as well as being beautiful, is also significant; that it is justified will be shown later. Those who wish to find another name only show that they have no inkling as to why the astral body is so named. In humans and animals, the astral body bestows on living substance the ability to experience sensation. This means that not only do currents of fluid move within it, but also sensations of joy, sorrow, pleasure and pain. This capacity constitutes the essential difference between plant and animal, although transitional stages between them do exist.

A certain group of scientists believes that sensation should be ascribed also to plants, but that is only playing with words. Certainly some plants do react when something approaches them, but it has nothing to do with sensation or feeling. When the latter is the case, an image arises within the creature in response to the stimulus. Even if certain plants respond to external stimuli, that is no proof that they experience inner sensation. The inwardly felt has its seat in the astral body. Thus, we see that creatures belonging to the animal kingdom consist of physical body, ether or life body, and astral body.

Human beings tower above the animal through a specific quality, often sensed by thoughtful natures. In his autobiography, Jean Paul[5] relates the deep impression made upon him when, as a small child, standing in the courtyard of his parent's house, the thought suddenly flashed through his mind: "I am an 'I,' I am a being who inwardly calls himself 'I.'" What is here described is of immense significance, yet generally overlooked by psychologists. A subtle observation will illustrate what is involved: In the whole range of speech, there is one small word that in its application differs from all others. We can all give a name to the objects in this room. Each one of us will call the table, "table," the chairs, "chairs," but there is one word, one name that can only refer to the one who speaks it: the little word "I." No one can call someone else "I." The word "I" must sound forth from the innermost soul to which it applies. To me, everyone else is a "you," and I am a "you" to everyone else.

Religions have recognized that the "I" is that principle in us that makes it possible for the human soul to express its innermost divine nature. With the "I" begins what can never enter the soul through the external senses, what must sound forth in its innermost being. It is where the monologue, the soliloquy, begins in which, if the path has been made clear for the spirit's entry, the divine Self may reveal itself.

In religions of earlier cultural epochs, and still in the Hebrew religion, the word "I" was called: "The unutterable name of God." No matter how it is interpreted according to modern philology, the ancient Hebrew name for God signifies what today is expressed by the word "I." A hush went through the assembly when the initiate spoke the "Name of the Unknown God"; the people would dimly sense the meaning contained in the words that resounded through the temple: "I am the I am."

Thus, the human being consists of physical body, ether body, astral body and the "I" or the essential inner being. This inner being contains within itself the germ of the three further evolutionary stages that will arise out of the blood. They are: Manas or Spirit Self, in contrast to the bodily self; Buddhi or Life Spirit; and a human's true spiritual being: Atma or Spirit Man, which today rests within us as a tiny seed to reach perfection in a far-off future; a stage to which at present we can only look to as a far-distant ideal. Therefore, just as we have seven colors in the rainbow and seven tones in the scale, we have seven members of our being that divide into four lower and three higher.

If we now look upon the three higher spiritual members as the "above" and the four lower as the "below," let us try to get a clear picture of how the above creates a physiognomic expression in the below as it appears to physical sight. Take first what we have in common with the whole inorganic nature, that is, that which crystallized into the form of a person's physical body. When we speak of the physical body in a spiritual-scientific sense, it is not what can be seen physically that is meant, but the combination of forces behind it that constructed this form. The next member of our being is the ether body, which plants and animals also possess, and by means of which they are endowed with life. The ether body transforms physical matter into living fluids, thus raising what is merely material into living form. In animal and human the ether body is permeated by the astral body, which calls up in the circulating fluid inner participation of its movement, causing the movement to be reflected inwardly.

We have now reached the point where the being of humans can be understood insofar as they are related to the animal kingdom. The substances, such as oxygen, nitrogen, hydrogen, sulphur, phosphorus, and so forth, out of which our physical body is composed, are to be found outside in inorganic nature. If the substances transformed by the ether body into living matter are to attain the capacity to create inner mirror images of external events, then the ether body must be permeated by the astral body. It is the astral body that gives rise to sensations and feelings, but at the animal level it does so in a specific way.

The ether body transforms inorganic substances into living fluids; the astral body transforms living substance into sensitive substance. But—and of this please take special note—a being composed of no more than the three bodies is only capable of sensing itself. It is only aware of its own life processes; its existence is confined within the boundaries of its own being. This fact is most interesting, and it is important to keep it in mind. Look for a moment at what has developed in a lower animal: inorganic matter is transformed into living substance, and living mobile substance into sensitive substance. The latter is to be found only where there is at least the rudiment of what at a higher stage becomes a developed nervous system.

Thus, we have inorganic substance, living substance, and nerve substance capable of sensation. In a crystal you see manifest certain laws of inorganic nature. (A crystal can be formed only within the whole surrounding nature.) No single entity could exist by itself separated from the rest of the cosmos. If we were to be transferred a mile or two above the earth's surface, we would die. Just as we are conceivable only within the environment to which we belong, where the necessary forces exist that combine to form and sustain us, so, too, in the case of a crystal. A person who knows how to look at a crystal will see it as an individual imprint of the whole of nature, indeed of the whole cosmos. Georges Leopold Chrètien Cuvier[6] is quite right when he says that a competent anatomist is able to deduce from a single bone to what kind of animal it belongs, as each kind has its own specific bone formation.

So you see that in the form of a crystal a certain aspect of the whole cosmos is reflected, just as an aspect of the whole cosmos is imprinted on living substance. The fluid circulating in a living creature is a small world that mirrors the great world. When substance possesses not only life, but also experiences inner sensation, it mirrors universal laws; it becomes a microcosm that dimly senses within itself the whole macrocosm. As the crystal is an image of cosmic form, so is sentient life an image of cosmic life. The dullness of consciousness in simple creatures is compensated by its immense range, for mirrored in it is the whole cosmos.

The constitution of humans is simply a more intricate structure composed of the three bodies already found in simple sentient creatures. If you consider people while disregarding their blood, you have beings built up from the same substances as those to be found in their environment. Like the plant, human beings contain fluids that call mineral substances to life, which in turn incorporate a system of nerves. The first nerves to appear are those of the so-called sympathetic nervous system. In humans it extends along both sides of the vertebral column, forming a series of knots from which it branches out and sends threads to the various organs, the lungs, the digestive tract and so on.

In the first instance, the sympathetic nervous system gives rise to the kind of sentient life just described. But a person's consciousness does not reach down far enough to experience the cosmic processes it mirrors. The surrounding cosmic world out of which the human being, as a living being, is created, mirrors itself in the sympathetic nervous system. There is in these nerves a dull inner life. If human beings could dive down consciously into the sympathetic nervous system, while the higher nervous system fell asleep, they would behold in a world of light the workings of the great cosmic laws.

Human beings once had a clairvoyant faculty that has been superseded. However, it can still be experienced, if through certain measures the function of the higher nervous system is suspended, setting free the lower consciousness. When that happens, the world is experienced through the lower nervous system in which the environment is mirrored in a special way. Certain lower animals still have this kind of consciousness. As explained, it is extremely dull, but provides a dim awareness of a far wider aspect of the world than the tiny section perceived by humans today.

At the time when evolution had reached the stage of the cosmos being mirrored in the sympathetic nervous system, another event occurred in human beings. The spinal cord was added to the sympathetic nervous system. The system of brain and spinal cord extended to the organs, through which contact was established with the outer world. Once their organisms had reached this stage, humans were no longer obliged to be merely a mirror for the primordial cosmic laws; the mirror image itself now entered into relationship with the environment. The incorporation of the higher nervous system in addition to the sympathetic nervous system denoted the transformation that had occurred in the astral body. Whereas formerly it participated dully in the life of the cosmos, it now contributed its own inner experiences.

Through the sympathetic nervous system, a being senses what takes place outside itself; through the higher nervous system, what takes place within itself. In individuals at the present stage of their evolution, the highest form of the nervous system is developed; it enables people to obtain from the highly structured astral body what is needed to formulate mental pictures of the outer world. Therefore, a person has lost the ability to experience the environment in the original dull pictures. Instead, individuals are aware of their inner life, and build within the inner self a new world of pictures on a higher level. This world of mental pictures mirrors, it is true, a much smaller section of the outer world, but does so much more clearly and perfectly.

Hand in hand with this transformation, another one occurred on a higher evolutionary level. The reorganization of the astral body became extended to the ether body. Just as the ether body through its reorganization became permeated with the astral body, and just as there was added to the sympathetic nervous system that of the brain and spinal cord, so what was set free from the ether body—after it had called into being the circulation of living fluids—now transformed these lower fluids into what we call "blood."

Blood denotes an individualized ether body, just as the brain and spinal cord denote an individualized astral body. And through this individualizing comes about that which expresses itself as the "I."

Having traced man's evolution up to this point, we notice that we are dealing with a gradation in five stages: First the physical body (or inorganic neutral physical forces); second the ether body (or living fluids, to be found also in plants); third the astral body (manifesting itself in the lower or sympathetic nervous system); fourth the higher astral body emerging from the lower astrality (manifesting itself in the brain and spinal cord); and finally the principle that individualizes the ether body.

Just as two of humanity's principles, the ether and astral bodies, have become individualized, so will the human being's first principle, built up out of external lifeless substances, that is, the physical body, become individualized. In present day humanity there is only a faint indication of this transformation.

We see that formless substances come together in the human body, that the ether body transforms them into living forms, that through the astral body the outer world is reflected and becomes inner sensation, and finally this inner life produces of itself pictures of the outer world.

When the process of transformation extends to the ether body, the result is the forming of blood. This transformation manifests itself in the system of heart and blood vessels, just as the transformation of the astral body manifests in the system of brain and spinal cord. And, as through the brain the outer world becomes inner world, so does this inner world become transformed through the blood into an outer manifestation as the human body. I shall have to speak in similes if I am to describe these complicated processes. The pictures of the external world made inward through the brain are absorbed by the blood and transformed into vital formative forces. These are the forces that build up the human body; in other words, blood is the substance that builds the body. We are dealing with a process that brings the blood into contact with the outer world; it enables it to take from it the most perfect substance, oxygen. Oxygen continually renews the blood, endowing it with new life.

In tracing human development, we have followed a path that leads from the outer world to humanity's inner world and back to the outer world. We have seen that the origin of blood coincides with our ability to face the world as an independent being, a being able to form his or her own pictures of the external world from its reflection within the self. Unless this stage is reached, a being cannot say "I" to itself. Blood is the principle whereby "I-hood" is attained. An "I" can express itself only in a being who is able independently to formulate the pictures the outer world produces within the self. A being who has attained "I-hood" must be able to take in the outer world and recreate it within the self.

If we possessed only a brain without a spinal cord, we would still reproduce within ourselves pictures of the outer world and be aware of them, but only as a mirror image. It is quite different when we are able to build up anew what is repeated within ourselves; for then what we thus build up is no longer merely pictures of the outer world; it is the "I." A being who possesses brain and spinal cord will not only mirror the outer world, as does a being with only the sympathetic nervous system, but will also experience the mirrored picture as inner life. A being who in addition possesses blood will experience inner life within the self. The blood, assisted by oxygen taken from the outer world, builds up the individual body according to the inner pictures. This is experienced as perception of the "I".

The "I" turns its vision inwards into a person's being, and its will outwards to the world. This twofold direction manifests itself in the blood, which directs its forces inwards, building up a person's being, and outwards towards the oxygen. When humans fall asleep they sink into unconsciousness because of what the consciousness experiences within the blood, whereas when they, by means of sense organs and brain, form mental pictures of the outer world, then the blood absorbs these pictures into its formative forces. Thus, the blood exists midway between an inner picture-world and an outer world of concrete forms. This becomes clearer if we look at two phenomena. One is that of genealogy, that is, the way conscious beings are related to ancestors, the other is the way we experience external events.

We are related to ancestors through the blood. We are born within a specific configuration, within a certain race, a certain family and from a certain line of ancestors. Everything inherited comes to expression in our blood. Likewise, all the results from an individual's physical past accumulates in the blood, just as within it there is prepared a prototype of that person's future. Consequently, when the individual's normal consciousness is suppressed, for example under hypnosis or in cases of somnambulism or atavistic clairvoyance, a much deeper consciousness becomes submerged. Then, in a dream-like fashion, the great cosmic laws are perceived. Yet this perception is nevertheless clearer than that of ordinary dreams even when lucid. In such conditions all brain activity is suppressed, and in deep somnambulism even that of the spinal cord. In this condition what the person experiences is conveyed by the sympathetic nervous system; the individual has a dull, hazy awareness of the whole cosmos. The blood no longer conveys mental pictures produced by the inner life through the brain; it only conveys what the outer world has built including everything inherited from ancestors. Just as the shape of a person's nose stems from his or her ancestors, so does the whole bodily form. In this state of consciousness a person senses his ancestors in the same manner that waking consciousness senses mental pictures of the outer world. A person's blood is haunted by his ancestors; he dimly participates in their existence.

Everything in the world evolves, also human consciousness. If we go back to the time when our remote ancestors lived, we find that they possessed a different type of consciousness. Today, during waking life we perceive external objects through the senses, and transform them into mental pictures that act on our blood. Everything a person experiences through the senses is working in not only his blood but also in his memory. By contrast, a person remains unconscious of everything bestowed by ancestors. We know nothing about the shape of our inner organs. In the past all this was different; at that time the blood conveyed not only what it received from outside through the senses, but also what existed in the bodily form, and as this was inherited, we could sense our ancestors within our own being.

If you imagine such a consciousness enhanced, you will get an idea of the kind of memory that corresponded to it. When our experiences are confined to what can be perceived through the senses, then only such senseperceptible experiences are remembered. A person's consciousness comprises only his experiences since childhood.

In the past this was different, because the inner life contained all that was brought over through heredity. A human's mental life depicted ancestors' experiences as if they were his own. A person could remember not only his own childhood, but his ancestors' lives, because they were contained in the pictures absorbed by his blood. Incredible as it may seem to the modern materialistic outlook, there was a time when human consciousness was such that an individual regarded both his and his forefathers' physical experiences as his own. When someone said: "I have experienced. . . ," he referred not only to personally known events but also to events experienced by his ancestors. It was a dim and hazy consciousness compared with modern human waking consciousness, more like a vivid dream. However, it was much more encompassing, as it included not only his own life but the lives of ancestors. A son would feel at one with his father and grandfather, as if they were sharing the same "I." This was also the reason he did not give himself a personal name but one that included past generations, designating what they had in common with one and the same name. Each person felt strongly that he was simply a link in a long line of generations.

The question is how this form of consciousness came to be transformed into a different one. It happened through an event well-known to spiritual historical research. You will find that every nation the world over describes a significant moment in history when a new phase of its culture began—the moment when the old traditions begin to lose their influence, and the ancient wisdom that had flowed down the generations via the blood begins to wane, although the wisdom still finds expression in myths and sagas.

A tribe used to be an enclosed unit; its members married among themselves. You will find this to be the case in all races and peoples. It was a significant moment in the history of mankind when this custom ceased to be upheld—the moment when a mingling of blood took place through the fact that marriage between close relations was replaced by marriage between strangers. Marriage within a tribe ensured that the same blood flowed through its members down the generations; marriage between strangers allowed new blood to be introduced into a people.

The tribal law of intermarriage will be broken sooner or later among all peoples. It heralds the birth of the intellect, which means ability to understand the external world, to understand what is foreign.

The important fact to bear in mind is that in ancient times a dim clairvoyance existed out of which arose sagas and legends, and that the clairvoyant consciousness is based on unmixed blood, whereas our awakened consciousness depends on mixed blood. Surprising as it may seem, marriage between strangers has resulted in logical, intellectual thoughts. This is a fact that will increasingly be confirmed by external research, which has already made a beginning in that direction. The mingling of blood extinguishes the former clairvoyance and enables humanity to reach a higher stage of evolution. When a person today goes through esoteric training and causes clairvoyance to reappear, that person transforms it to a higher consciousness, whereas today's waking consciousness has evolved out of the ancient dim clairvoyance.

In our time, a person's whole surrounding world in which he acted came to expression in the blood;

consequently, this surrounding world formed the inner in accordance with the outer. In ancient times it was more a person's inner bodily life that came to expression in the blood. A person inherited, along with the memory of his ancestors' experiences, also their good or bad inclinations; these could be traced in his blood. This ancestral bond was severed when blood became mingled through outside marriages. The individual began to live his own personal life; he learned to govern his moral inclinations according to his own experiences. Thus, ancestral power holds sway in unmixed blood; that of personal experience in mixed blood.

Myths and legends told of these things: "That which has power over thy blood has power over thee." Ancestral power over a folk came to an end when the blood, through being mingled with foreign blood, ceased to be receptive to its influence. This held good in all circumstances.

Whatever power wishes to subjugate a person will have to exert an influence that imprints itself in his blood. Thus, if an evil power wishes dominance over an individual, it must gain dominance over his or her blood. That is the profound meaning of the quotation from *Faust*, and the reason the representative of evil says: "Sign your name to the pact in blood; once I possess your name written in your blood, I shall have caught you by the one thing that will hold man. I shall then be able to pull you over to my side." That which possesses a person's blood possesses that person, and possesses the human "I. "

When two groups of human beings confront one another, as used to be the case in colonization, then only if there is true insight into evolutionary laws is there any possibility of foreseeing if the foreign culture can be assimilated. Take the case of a people that is very much at one with its environment, a people into whose blood the environment has as it were inserted itself. No attempt to graft upon it a foreign culture will succeed. It is simply impossible, and is also the reason why in certain regions the original inhabitants became extinct when colonized. One must approach such problems with insight and realize that anything and everything cannot be forced upon a people. It is useless to demand of blood more than it is able to endure.

Modern science has discovered recently that if blood from one animal is mixed with that of another not akin to it, the two types of blood prove fatal to one another. This is something that has been known to spiritual knowledge for a long time. Just as unrelated types of blood if mixed cause death, so is the old clairvoyance killed in primitive humanity when blood from different lines of descent are mingled. Our modern intellectual life is entirely the outcome of the mingling of blood. Once this approach is adopted it will be possible to study what effect the mingling of blood has had on the various people in the course of history.

Thus, when the blood of animals from different evolutionary stages is mixed the result is death, whereas that is not the case when the species are related. The human organism survives when, through marriage, blood is mingled with strange blood; here the result is the extinction of the original animal kind of clairvoyance, and the birth in evolution of a new consciousness. In other words, something happens in humans, but on a higher level, that is similar to what happens in the animal kingdom where strange blood kills strange blood. In the human kingdom strange blood kills the hazy clairvoyance that is based on kindred blood.

Therefore, it is a destructive process that gave rise to the modern human wakeful day-consciousness. The kind of spiritual life that resulted from intermarriage has been destroyed in the course of evolution; while the very thing that destroyed it, that is, marriage between strangers, gave birth to the intellect and today's lucid consciousness.

What is able to live in a person's blood lives in that person's "I." Just as the physical principle comes to expression in the physical body, the ether body comes to expression in the system of living fluids, and the astral body in the system of nerves, so does the "I" come to expression in the blood. Physical principle, ether body and astral body are the "above" blood; the "I" forms the center; and physical body, living fluids and nervous system are the "below." Therefore, whatever power wishes to dominate humans must take possession of their blood.

These are things that must be taken into account if progress is to be achieved in practical life. For example, just because the "I" comes to expression in the blood, a people's racial character can be destroyed through colonization, when more is demanded than the blood can endure.

Not till Beauty and Truth become part of a person's blood does he truly possess them. Mephistopheles wants power over Faust's "I"; that is why he seizes Faust's blood. So you see that the quotation, which is the leitmotiv of this lecture, arose out of profound knowledge. *Blood is indeed a very special fluid.*

Lecture III

The Origin of Suffering

Berlin, November 8, 1906

Today's lecture has a close connection with the two succeeding discourses entitled, "The Origin of Evil"; and "Illness and Death." Yet each lecture is complete and comprehensible by itself.

Someone who contemplates his own life, as well as life in general, encounters at the outset, like an enigmatic figure standing guard before life's portal, the problem of suffering.

Suffering, so closely bound up with evil, illness and death, often cuts deeply into people's lives, and is seen as one of its greatest riddles. When attempts are made to find meaning in life, to assess its value, it is above all pain and suffering that come under scrutiny. In all world views since ancient times, it features as one of the foremost questions.

Suffering appears like an unwelcome intruder; it destroys, in the midst of happiness, enjoyment and hope. People who feel pain and suffering the most are those that measure life's value according to its pleasures, that, as it were, exist solely for the sake of enjoyment. It explains why a people as happy and as full of enjoyment of life as the ancient Greeks had a saying which hung like a dark cloud in the midst of the beautiful stars on the Hellenic firmament. The wise Silenus[1], a member of Dionysus'[2] retinue, answers the question, What is best for man? by saying: "The best for man is not to be born, and if born the next best for him is to die soon after."

As you may know, Friedrich Nietzsche[3] occupied himself with this saying in his effort to understand the birth of tragedy out of the spirit of ancient Greece. He wanted to demonstrate, on the basis of Greek art and philosophy, the significant role played by suffering itself, and the sorrow it caused. However, not much later another saying came to the fore in Greece that shows a dawning understanding for the fact that the significance of pain goes far beyond that of misfortune. We find in Aeschylus,[4] one of the early Greek tragic poets, the saying, "From suffering knowledge is born." Two things are here brought together, one of which the greater part of humanity would no doubt prefer to see eliminated, while seeing in the other one of life's greatest benefits.

From time immemorial, the belief has existed that life on this planet is unavoidably entwined with suffering, at least as far as human beings and the higher creatures are concerned–a view we find expressed at the start of the biblical story of creation, where knowledge of good and evil is intimately bound up with suffering. However, we also find in the Old Testament the view expressed that there can dawn, within the bleakest outlook caused by suffering, one filled with hope and light. A closer look at the Old Testament makes it clear that right from ancient times, sin and suffering have always been seen as connected, suffering as being a consequence of sin. The modern materialistic outlook finds it difficult to grasp that suffering may originate from sin. But when one has learned through spiritual research to look back into earlier ages, one recognizes that this view is not without foundation; the next lecture will show that it is possible to connect evil and suffering.

But in one case ancient Judaism found it impossible to explain the origin of suffering. In the midst of views connecting suffering with sin, we find the remarkable figure of Job. The story of Job shows, or is meant to show, that undeserved suffering can exist, that unspeakable pain can come about in a life without sin. In the uniquely tragic personality of Job, we see a dawning consciousness of a different connection, namely, a connection between suffering and ennoblement. Here suffering appears as a testing, as an incentive to greater striving. In the sense of Job's tragedy, suffering need not originate from evil; it may be a first cause from which will result a more perfect phase in human life. This viewpoint is rather remote from the modern way of thinking; most of today's educated people would find it difficult to accept. But if you look back over your life you will realize how often suffering and higher development go together. Furthermore, humanity has always been aware of this connection; and that leads us to today's subject. We shall consider in the sense of spiritual science the connection between suffering and spirituality.

In dramas the central figure is often the tragic hero. The hero is faced again and again with suffering and conflict; at last at the climax the suffering ends with the death of the physical body. At this point the onlooker not only experiences compassion for the tragic hero and sorrow that such suffering exists; but he also has gone through a catharsis, and feels that from death certainty arises, certainty that pain and suffering, and even death itself, are conquered.

No art form portrays more sublimely than the tragedy the greatest human victory, the victory of a person's innermost and noblest forces. On the stage we can often witness the conquest of pain and suffering. It is brought forcefully to our consciousness when we contemplate the event recognized by a large part of humanity as the greatest in history. The event that divides our reckoning of time into two parts—the salvation through Christ Jesus. It may strike us that, precisely through contemplating a suffering of world magnitude, the profoundest hope takes root in human hearts. Christianity reassures us concerning eternity, concerning victory over death. From looking up to a universal suffering preceded by no personal guilt or sin, we derive hope and strength. This indicates a consolatory feeling in the human soul that always asserts itself in the face of suffering.

If we look at human life more carefully, we find phenomena that indicate the significance of suffering. Let us look at one such phenomenon that is symptomatic, although at first sight it may not appear to be connected with suffering.

Think once more of a tragedy. The poet can only create such a work of art if he has the capacity to go out of himself, to widen his soul and encompass the suffering of others. The poet must be able to experience the suffering of others as if it were his own. But now compare this attitude with a very different one–not however with what inspires comedy–that would not be the right comparison. Rather compare it with the attitude that inspires caricature; that too in a sense belongs to the realm of art. The caricaturist distorts what is expressed outwardly of what lives in another soul, perhaps with ridicule and derision. Let us now imagine two persons, one of whom sees an event or a human being as tragic, the other who sees the situation in caricature. It is no mere simile when we say that the artist as tragic poet goes out of himself, allowing his soul to become ever more encompassing. But what is it that individuals attain through this ever widening of their inner being? They attain understanding of the other. Nothing provides greater understanding than experiencing another person's suffering as one's own. But what about the caricaturist? He cannot enter into the other person's feeling; on the contrary, he must reject, must set himself above it. The refusal to consider the other person's inner life is basic to caricature. No one can fail to see that compassion leads to understanding of the other, whereas caricature reveals the nature of the caricaturist. We learn through his work far more about his feeling of superiority, wit, and power of observation and imagination, than we learn about the nature of his subject.

If these examples make it evident that suffering is connected with deeper aspects of human nature, it is to be hoped that an understanding of our essential nature will also make clear how pain and suffering originate.

Spiritual science recognizes that the whole physical world about us originated from the spirit, whereas the materialistic view only sees spirit where it appears as a kind of crown on physical material creation, as a kind of flower growing from physical roots. The materialistic view sees, as it were, the inorganic organizing itself within the living creatures. Consciousness, pleasure and pain emerge from sentient life, the spirit from the corporeal. When the spiritual researcher looks at the way spirit first appears in the natural world, he too sees it emerging from the physical.

We saw in the preceding two lectures that in the light of spiritual science we must think of the human being as consisting not only of a physical or bodily nature, but also of soul and spirit. What materialism regards as the whole of existence, that is, what can be perceived physically, spiritual science maintains is in man only his first member: the physical body. We know it is built up from the same substances as those that exist in inorganic nature, but we also know that it is called into life by the so-called ether or life body. This ether body is not something merely thought out; it is a reality and can be perceived when the higher senses that slumber in us are developed. The ether body is the second member of our being, also possessed by the vegetable kingdom. Our third member, the astral body, is the bearer of pleasure and pain, cravings and passions; animals also possess an astral body. In the human being we see emerging within his physical, ether and astral bodies conscious-ness of self, that is, the ability to call himself "I." This is the crown of his nature, which no other earthly being possesses. Spiritual science has often indicated the interrelation of these four members. The Pythagorean fourfoldness is nothing else than that of physical body, ether body, astral body and "I." Those who have gone more deeply into spiritual science know that the "I" of a human being will develop out of itself what is termed: Spirit Self or Manas; Life Spirit or Buddhi; and Spirit Man or Atma, an individual's essential spirit being. This is all mentioned again today to ensure proper orienta-tion.

Thus, the spiritual investigator sees the human being as a fourfold being. At a certain point spiritual research differs decisively from external research because spiri-tual perception penetrates deeply into the foundation of existence. However, the spiritual investigator also sees that, as a human being comes before us in the physical world, physical matter and laws constitute the foundation of a person's bodily nature; life constitutes the foundation of sensation; and consciousness the foundation of self-consciousness. But to spiritual research the sequence is seen the other way round. What to physical appearance seems to be the last to emerge from the physical body, that is, consciousness, is seen by the spiritual investigator as the primordial creative element. The conscious spirit is seen as the foundation of all existence. Consequently one cannot ask, Where does spirit come from? That can never be the question, rather, Where does matter come from? Spiritual research shows that matter originates from spirit; it is nothing but condensed spirit.

One might compare the process with water condensing into ice. Think of a vessel with water, part of which has cooled to below freezing so that ice has formed. This ice is nothing but water in solid form. Spirit relates to matter as water to ice. As ice can become water once more, so can spirit emerge again from matter, or conversely, matter can dissolve into spirit.

Thus, we see spirit in eternal circulation. Out of spirit that fills the whole universe, we see material entities arise and solidify; on the other hand material entities continually dissolve again. Spirit has flowed into everything that surrounds us as matter. Everything material is solidified spirit. Just as we only have to add the necessary heat for ice to turn back into water, so it is only necessary to add enough spirit to the physical beings to make the spirit resurrect in them. One speaks of a rebirth of the spirit which, having flowed into matter, has become solidified. Thus, we see that the astral body, the bearer of pleasure and pain, cravings and passions, is something that could not possibly originate from the physical. It is of the same element that permeates the whole world, but in us it lives as conscious spirit. It will be released from matter through the processes that govern human life. The spirit that in the physical world appears as the last is at the same time the first. The spirit brings the physical body and the ether body into existence, and when these have reached a certain point in their evolution, the spirit reappears as if reborn within them.

Physical substance, matter, we always perceive in a certain shape, in a certain form. We speak of material form, of life that arises within that form, and of consciousness arising within the living form. Thus, we speak of the three stages: physical body, ether body and astral body, and also of the three corresponding stages: form, life and consciousness. Not until the stage of consciousness is reached can self-consciousness arise. This will concern us in the next lecture.

The meaning and origin of life have always been subjects of much discussion, not least in our time. Modern natural science has not discovered many points of reference in this field. However, natural science has recently arrived at a conclusion that spiritual science has always maintained, namely, that organic and inorganic substances do not differ as far as the actual substances are concerned. The only difference lies in the fact that organic substances are more complex in their composition. Life can arise only where there are substances of varied and complex structure. As you may know, the basic substance where there is life is a white-of-egg-like substance which could well be called "living albumen." It has one important characteristic that makes it differ from lifeless albumen; it begins to deteriorate the moment life has left it. That is why eggs, for example, do not stay fresh for long. The essential character of living substance is that it cannot remain a unity once life has departed.

Although we cannot today go into detail about the nature of life, we can consider this one essential characteristic of living substance, the fact that it disintegrates the moment life has gone from it. A complex structure composed of various substances will disintegrate if not permeated with life. That is its most characteristic feature. So what does life do? It preserves, it continuously opposes disintegration. Life has the ability to rejuvenate because it continuously opposes what would otherwise take place in substances it permeates. When a substance contains life it means that disintegration is being fought. Life possesses the exact opposite qualities to those of death; instead of causing substances to fall apart, it continually holds them together. Thus, life becomes the foundation of physical existence and consciousness by constantly preventing disintegration.

This is not just a verbal definition; what it points to happens all the time. You only have to observe the simplest form of life and you will find that substances are perpetually being absorbed and incorporated while bodily particles deteriorate; it is the latter process that life continuously works against. Thus, we are dealing with an actual phenomenon.

Life means that new substances are formed and old ones thrown off. But life is not yet either sensation or consciousness. Certain scientists fail to understand sensation and ascribe it to plants that have life but not sensation. This childish notion comes about because there are plants that close their leaves and blossoms in response to external stimuli. One could just as well ascribe sensation to blue litmus paper that turns red in response to external stimuli, or to chemical substances as they too react to certain influences. But that is not enough.

If sensation is to occur, there must be an inner mirroring of the stimulus; only then can we speak of the lower form of consciousness, sensation and feeling. But what exactly is it? If we are to gain insight into this next higher stage of evolution, we must approach it gradually as we did the nature of life. Consciousness arises from life; it can only come into being where life already exists. It reveals itself as higher than life; the latter seemingly arises out of lifeless matter of such complexity that unless seized by life it disintegrates. Consciousness arises at the border between life and death, that is to say, where life constantly threatens to disappear from substance, and where substance is continually being destroyed. Substance disintegrates unless held together by forces of life. Life dissolves unless a new principle, that is, consciousness, is added. Consciousness can only be understood when it is recognized that it constantly renews life that would otherwise dissolve, just as life forces renew certain processes without which matter would decay.

Not every form of life can renew itself from within. It must first have reached a certain higher level. Only when the force of life is strong enough constantly to endure death within itself can it awake to consciousness. To be aware of life that at every moment contains death, you need only look at life within the human being, and bear in mind what was explained in the last lecture, "Blood is a very special Fluid," and that within human beings, life is constantly renewed through the blood. As a psychologist with insight remarked: "In the blood man carries within him a double from whom he constantly draws strength." But blood contains yet another force: it continuously produces death. When it has taken life-giving substances to the organs, it carries away destructive elements back to the heart and lungs.

What returns to the lungs is poisonous, destructive to life.

A being whose nature works against disintegration is a being possessing life. If it is able to let death arise, and continuously transform that death into life, then it is a conscious being. Consciousness is the strongest of all forces. Death must of necessity arise in the midst of life; consciousness, or conscious spirit, is the force that eternally wrenches life from death. Life is both an inward and an external process, whereas consciousness is a purely an inward one. A substance that dies outwardly cannot become conscious. Consciousness can only arise in substance that can generate death within itself and overcome it. As a perceptive person once remarked: "From death springs not only life but consciousness."

Once this connection is recognized, the existence of pain becomes comprehensible. It is pain that originally gave rise to consciousness. When the life within a being is exposed to light, air, heat or cold, then these external elements act in the first place on the living being. This influence does not give rise to consciousness in plants because here the effects are simply absorbed. Consciousness only arises when there is conflict between the external elements and the inner life-force, causing a breaking down of tissue. Consciousness can only arise from the inner destruction of life. Unless a partial death takes place in the living being, the process that gives rise to consciousness cannot be initiated; beams of light cannot penetrate to the surface of life, causing partial destruction of the inner substances and forces. It is this that produces the mysterious process that is occurring everywhere in the external world.

You must visualize that the cosmic forces of intelligence had reached a level of evolution so high that the external light and air became alien. There had been harmony for a time, but through the higher perfection of cosmic forces, conflict arose. If you could follow with spiritual sight what happens at the point where a simple living creature is penetrated by a beam of light, you would see alteration in the skin; a tiny eye begins to appear. A delicate form of destruction occurs that is experienced as pain. From this pain consciousness is born. Wherever the element of life meets the external world, a process of destruction occurs; if great enough, the outcome is death. The pain gives rise to consciousness. The process that originally created our eyes could have resulted in complete destruction had it gained the upper hand. But it seized upon only a small part of the human being, and through partial destruction, partial death created the possibility for that inner reflection of the outer world to arise that we call "consciousness." Thus, consciousness within matter is born out of suffering and pain.

When this connection between pain and the conscious spirit around us is recognized, many things become comprehensible, for example, why thoughtful people ascribe such a significant role to pain. An important philosopher has pointed out that an expression of suffering and pain is to be seen everywhere on the countenance of the world. Indeed, the physiognomy of the higher animals conveys deeply repressed pain.

Thus, we see that consciousness comes into existence through pain, that a being in whom consciousness arises from destruction creates from the annihilation of life something that is higher, and in fact continuously creates itself out of death. If the living could not suffer, consciousness could not arise; if there were no death, the spirit could not exist in the visible world. Herein lies the strength of the spirit: It creates from destruction something higher than life, namely, consciousness. We see the organs serving consciousness develop at different levels of pain. This can be observed already in the lower animal kingdom where the level of consciousness, in defense against the outer world, consists of instinctive reflex movements, comparable to the human eye instinctively closing itself against what might harm it. It is when such instinctive reaction is not enough to protect the element of life in the creature, when in other words the provocation is too strong, that the inner forces of opposition are roused which in turn give birth to senses, to sensation, and to organs like the eye and ear. You may have an instinctive feeling that what I have just explained is the truth. You certainly know it in your higher consciousness, but let me give you an example to make it clearer still. When do you become aware of your inner organs? You go through life paying no attention to your stomach, liver or lungs. You feel none of your organs as long as they are sound. You only know that you possess this or that organ when it hurts, when you feel something is out of order, in other words, when destruction has set in. This illustrates that consciousness always arises from pain.

If the element of life meets with pain, the result is sensation and consciousness. This bringing forth of a higher element is reflected in the consciousness as pleasure. No pleasure exists without prior pain. At the lower level, where life is just emerging within physical substance, no pleasure exists as yet. But when pain has given rise to consciousness, and as consciousness continues to work creatively, what it then produces is on a higher level, and gives rise to feelings of pleasure. Creativeness is the basis of pleasure. Pleasure only exists where there is a possibility for inner or outer creativity. Happiness is always in some way based on creation, just as unhappiness is in some way due to the need to create. Take an example of suffering that is typical on a lower level, that of hunger which can result in destruction of life. Hunger is alleviated by food; the food is a source of enjoyment because it becomes transformed into something that enhances life. Thus, something higher, namely, pleasure is created on the basis of pain. Suffering precedes pleasure. Thus, it must be said that while Arthur Schopenhauer[5] and Eduard von Hartmann[6] are right when they state in their philosophic work that suffering is a universal factor of life, they do not go deeply enough into the origin of suffering. They do not go back to the point where suffering evolves and becomes something higher. The origin of suffering is found where consciousness arises out of the element of life, where life gives birth to spirit.

We have shown that from suffering something nobler and more perfect is born. It is therefore comprehensible that an inkling should dawn in human souls for the fact that a connection exists between pain and suffering on the one hand, and knowledge and consciousness on the other.

Those who are acquainted with my lectures will recall references to initiation by means of which a higher consciousness is attained that enables us to perceive the spiritual world. When a person's slumbering soul forces and faculties are awakened, the result is comparable to sight being restored to someone born blind. Just as such a person will experience the whole world differently, so the whole world is transformed for the human being who has attained spiritual sight. Everything is seen in a new light and on a higher level. But for this to come about, the process that has been explained must be repeated at a higher stage. The soul forces that generally speaking from a unity in humans must separate; a kind of destruction must take place in a person's lower nature. Only when this occurs is a higher consciousness and spiritual perception attained.

There are three soul forces in human beings: thinking, feeling and willing. These three forces are bound up with the physical organization. Certain thoughts and feelings will call up certain acts of will. The human organism must function correctly if the three soul forces are to act in harmony. If the connection between them has broken down due to illness, then there is no longer consistency between thinking, feeling and willing. If an organ connected with the will is impaired, the human being will be unable to translate his thoughts into impulses of will; he is weak as far as action is concerned. Although a person is well able to think, he cannot decide on action. Another disturbance may be that someone is unable to link thoughts and feelings correctly; this human cannot bring his feelings into harmony with the thoughts behind them. Basically that is the cause of insanity.

In the normally constituted human being of today, thinking, feeling and willing are in harmony. This is right at certain stages of evolution. However, it must be born in mind that as far as a person is concerned, this harmony is established unconsciously. If a person is to be initiated, if he or she is to become capable of higher perception, then thinking, feeling and willing must be severed from one another. The organs connected with feeling and will must undergo division. Consequently, even if it cannot be proved anatomically, the organism of an initiate is different from that of a non-initiate. Because the contact between thinking, feeling and willing is severed, the initiate can see someone suffering without his feelings being roused; he can stand aside and coldly observe. The reason is that nothing must occur in the initiate unconsciously. An individual is compassionate out of his own free will, not because of some external compulsion. He becomes separated into human beings of feeling, a person of will and a thinking person; above these three is the ruler, the newfound individual, bringing them into harmony from a higher consciousness. Here too a death process, a destructive process must intervene; should this occur without a higher consciousness being attained, insanity would set in. Insanity is in fact a condition in which the three soul members have separated without being ruled by a higher consciousness.

Here too we see a twofold event taking place: a destructive process at work in what is lower, simultaneous with the creation of a higher element. The ordinary person's consciousness lights up between blue, poisonous, destructive blood, and red, life-giving blood; similarly the initiate's higher consciousness is born from the interaction of life and death, and bliss arises from the higher happiness of creating out of death.

Human beings have an instinctive feeling for that mysterious connection between the highest they can attain, and suffering, and pain. This feeling inspires the tragic poet to let the suffering to which his hero succumbs give rise to the conviction that ultimately life triumphs over death; the eternal over the temporal. Thus, Christianity rightly sees in the pain and suffering, in the anguish and misery to which Christ Jesus' earthly nature succumbs, the victory of eternal life over the temporal and transitory. It is also the reason why our life becomes richer, more satisfying, when we can widen it so that we absorb and make our own what lies beyond our own self.

When we, as beings possessing life, overcame the pain caused by the beam of external light, something higher was born, that is, consciousness. Likewise, something higher is born from receptiveness to suffering when we, in our widened consciousness, transform out of compassion the suffering of another into our own. Therefore, at the highest level suffering gives rise to love. For what else is love than widening one's consciousness to encompass other beings? It is love when we are willing to deprive ourselves, to sacrifice ourselves to whatever extent for the sake of another. Like the skin that received the beam of light, and out of the pain became able to create a higher entity: the eye; so will we, through widening our life to encompass the lives of others, become able to attain a higher life. There will then, out of what we have given away to others, be born within us love and compassion for all creatures.

The death on the cross of Christ Jesus bears witness to this truth, for, as Christianity teaches, there soon followed the outpouring of the Holy Spirit. In the light of the process we have explained, which is indicated in the parable of the grain of wheat, we can now understand the coming forth of the Holy Spirit as a consequence of the death on the Cross. Just as the new crop of wheat must rise from the decay, the destruction of the seeds; so from the destruction, the pain endured upon the Cross, that Spirit is born which poured out over the Apostles at the feast of Pentecost. This is clearly stated in the Gospel of John 7:39, where it is said that the Spirit was not yet there, for Christ was not yet glorified. To read the Gospel of John closely is to discover things of immense significance.

Many people say that they would not want to be spared the pain they have endured, for from it they have gained knowledge. This is a truth that those who have died would confirm. If pain did not stand constantly at our side, like a guardian of life, the destruction that goes on within us would lead to actual death. It is pain that warns us we must take precaution to prevent life being destroyed; thus, from pain comes new life. As mentioned, a modern natural scientist describes the mimicry of thinking as the expression of suppressed pain on a thinker's face.

If we learn through pain, if knowledge attained through pain has an ennobling effect, then it explains why in the biblical story of creation pain and suffering are connected with the knowledge of good and evil. This we shall go into in the next lecture. It also explains why knowledgeable people have always emphasized that pain has an ennobling, purifying effect on a person. Through the great law of destiny, karma, spiritual science indicates that a person's pain and suffering in one life point to wrong done in former lives. This is a connection that can only be understood through the deeper aspects of human nature. Baser impulses that in a former life led to external action are transformed into nobler ones. Sin is like a poison that when transformed becomes a source of healing. Thus, sin can eventually contribute to a person's strength and ennoblement. In the story of Job, pain and suffering are shown to lead to greater knowledge and ennoblement.

This is meant only as a sketch, as an indication of the significance of suffering in earthly existence. When we recognize the solidifying, crystallizing effect of pain in physical entities right up to that of human beings, then we begin to realize the reason for its existence—especially when we further recognize that through dissolving what has hardened, the spirit can be reborn through us, that through the transformation of pain and suffering the spirit bestows upon us beauty, strength and wisdom. Fabre d'Olivet used the formation of a pearl when he wished to illustrate that the highest, noblest and purest in human nature is born from pain. The precious and beautiful pearl is created from the illness and pain of the pearl-oyster. The highest and noblest qualities of human nature are attained through suffering and pain.

Thus, we may say, as did the ancient Greek poet Aeschylus, that from suffering knowledge is born, and also that pain, like much else, can be understood only by its fruits.

Lecture IV

The Origin of Evil

Berlin, November 22, 1906

It is characteristic of today's literature that it hardly mentions evil. Materialism may appear to have explanations for suffering, illness and death, but does not concern itself with evil. In the animal kingdom one can speak of ferocity and cruelty, but one cannot apply the concept of evil to animals. Evil is confined to the human kingdom. But modern natural science tries to derive knowledge of human beings from investigations of animals, and as all differences are glossed over, evil is ignored. One has to enter deeply into human characteristics in order to discover the origin of evil. One must above all recognize that humanity constitutes a kingdom by itself. Let us now consider this issue in the light of spiritual science.

There exists a primordial human wisdom that penetrates beneath the surface to the essence of things. It used to be preserved within narrow circles to which no one was admitted except after strict tests. The guardian of the wisdom had to be convinced that the one seeking entry would only use the knowledge for selfless purposes. During the last decades the elementary aspects of this wisdom-science are being made public; there are certain reasons why this is happening. It will increasingly flow into everyday life; we are at the beginning of this development.

But what is the connection between human beings' essential nature and evil? Various attempts have been made to explain evil. Some say that there is no evil as such, only an absence of good; evil is supposed to be the lowest degree of good. Others say that just as good is an original force, so is evil. The Persian legend of Ormuzd and Ahriman emphasizes this view more especially. Spiritual science is the first to show that to understand evil one must enter deeply into the nature of human beings, and indeed into that of the whole cosmos. To deny its existence as such is to close the door to any comprehension of evil. We must look at how human beings evolved in the past and will evolve in the future, and thereby seek to discover the task, the mission of evil in the world.

Spiritual science points to the fact that there are highly developed individuals called the "initiates." In every age there have been secret schools where it was taught how, through exercises in meditation and concentration, a person could reach higher stages of development. Such exercises lead to insight that cannot be attained by means of the five senses and the intellect. Inner meditative work enables the soul to become free of the senses; something occurs in an individual that is comparable to what happens in someone born blind and whose sight is restored. An inner process takes place through which the spiritual eyes and ears are opened. The whole of humanity will reach this stage, but only after long periods of time. It is essential that those who seek higher development in no way neglect worldly, everyday affairs; the ascetic who flees the world will not attain spiritual vision, for the new clairvoyance is the fruit of the soul's experiences gathered in the physical world. The Greek philosophers have compared the human soul to the bee gathering honey, saying that the world of color and light offers honey to the human soul, to carry it up to higher worlds. The task of the human soul is to spiritualize sense experiences and take them up to higher worlds.

But what is its task once the soul becomes free of the body? Here we touch on a fundamental and significant law: Whenever beings reach a higher stage of evolution, they become the leaders and guides of the beings belonging to the forms of existence they have themselves passed through. When a person has become spiritualized, and no longer needs a physical body, he will attain spiritual leadership and work on a new planet from outside. By then our present planet will have fulfilled its mission and passed over into another embodiment. A new planetary existence will arise, and humanity will be gods on that planet. The human bodily nature, forsaken by the spirit, will constitute a lower kingdom. Human nature is already twofold, consisting of that which will rule on the next planet, and that which will be a lower kingdom. The earth will pass over into a new embodiment, just as it has passed through earlier ones. Human beings will be gods on the next planet, just as the beings that now lead us were human beings on the previous planet. This illustrates how the earth is connected with the past and the future. The Elohim, the creators and leaders of human evolution, were once at the stage we have reached on the earth. On the future planet human beings will have advanced to be leaders and guides.

However, it must not be thought that the same repeats itself; nothing ever happens twice. Never before has there been an existence like ours. Earth evolution represents the cosmos of love; the previous planet the cosmos of wisdom. On the earth love is to develop from the most elementary stage to the loftiest.

Wisdom, though hidden, permeates the foundation of earth existence; consequently, we ought not to speak of a person's physical nature as "lower," for it is in reality the most perfect aspect of his being. To recognize it one only has to look at the wisdom-filled bone structure, such as the upper thigh bone. Here we find the perfect solution to the problem: how the least expenditure of material can be structured to carry the maximum weight, or think of the wonderful forms of heart and brain. The astral body most certainly is not at a higher stage; it is the *bon viveur* that continually attacks the wise form of the heart. The astral body will need long ages to become as perfect and as wise as the physical body, though it will do so in the course of evolution. The physical body has gone through a corresponding development; it has evolved from unwisdom and error to wisdom.

Wisdom developed before love; as yet love is far from perfect, but even now it is to be found at all levels of existence, in plant, animal and human beings, from the lowest sexual love to the highest spiritualized love. Untold numbers of beings who have developed the urge for love are destroyed in the struggle for existence. Where there is love there is conflict, but love will overcome the conflict and transform it into harmony.

The characteristic of physical nature is wisdom; the evolution of the earth began when wisdom became permeated by love. As today there is conflict on earth, so there were errors on the previous planet. Peculiar legendary creatures wandered about, mistakes of nature incapable of evolution. Just as love evolves from non-love, so wisdom evolves from unwisdom. Those who attain the goal of earth evolution will bring love over to the next planet, as wisdom was originally brought over into the earth evolution. Earthly humanity looks up to the gods as bringers of wisdom; the humanity on the next planet will look up to the gods as bringers of love. On earth, wisdom is vouchsafed to human beings as divine revelation through beings who were humans on the previous planet. Thus, all realms are interlinked. If there were no plants, the air would soon be polluted. Plants give off life-giving oxygen inhaled by human beings and animals, who in turn exhale carbonic acid that would destroy the air were it not inhaled by the plants. In this respect, the higher depends on the lower for the very breath of life.

This interdependence applies to all stages and kingdoms. Just as humans and animals depend on the world of plants, so do the gods depend upon mortals. Greek mythology expresses this poetically, saying that from the mortals the gods receive nectar and ambrosia, both words meaning love. Love comes into existence through humans, and love is food for the gods. The love engendered by mortals is breathed in by the gods. This may seem very strange, yet it is a fact more real than, say, electricity. At first love appears as sexual love and evolves to the highest spiritual love, but all love, the highest as well as the lowest, is the breath of gods. It might be said: If this is so then there can be no evil. But it must be remembered that, just as wisdom is born of error, so love can only evolve and reach perfection through conflict. However, love will be guided by the wisdom that is the foundation of the world.

Not all the beings on the previous planet attained the height of wisdom. Some remained behind and are at a level of development between gods and humans.

71

Though they still need something from human beings, they can no longer clothe themselves in physical bodies. They are designated as Luciferian beings, or collectively by the name of their leader—Lucifer. Lucifer's influence on human beings is very different from that of the gods. The gods approach what is noblest in human nature; a mortal's lower nature they cannot and must not approach. Only at the end of evolution can wisdom and love be united. The Luciferian beings approach a person's lower nature, the undeveloped element of love, they build a bridge between wisdom and love, thus causing a mingling of the two, with the result that what should remain impersonal becomes entangled with what is personal.

Wisdom was instinctive on the previous planet, as love is instinctive now. On the previous planet, a creative instinct of wisdom ruled, as now a creative instinct of love. Thus, human beings were formerly guided by instinctive wisdom; then it withdrew its guidance, and we became conscious and aware of ourselves as independent beings.

We are told in the story of Paradise: ". . . and they saw that they were naked." That means that human beings saw themselves for the first time; previously they had seen only the external world. They had earth-consciousness, but no self-consciousness. The latter enabled them to put wisdom into the service of the self. From then onwards there existed not only selfless love for the surrounding world, but also love of self; the former was good, the latter was bad.

Without Lucifer, human self-consciousness would never have become mingled with love. Thinking and wisdom now became servants of the self; a person could choose between good and evil. But love ought to be directed to the self only in order to place it in the service of the world: The rose should adorn itself only to adorn the garden. That must be deeply engraved in the hearts of those who seek higher development. In order to have a feeling for what is good, we must also have a feeling for what is bad. The gods endowed us with enthusiasm for what is higher; but without evil we would have no feeling of self, no free choice of the good, no freedom.

The good could have become reality without Lucifer, but not freedom. In order to choose the good, we must also have the evil before us; it must exist within us as self-love. When the force of self-love has developed and widened to become love of all, evil will be overcome. Evil and freedom stem from the same original source. Lucifer kindled human enthusiasm for the divine. He is the Light-bearer; the Elohim are the Light itself. Lucifer brought light into human beings by kindling in them the light of wisdom, albeit mingled with the black shadow of evil. The wisdom Lucifer brings is shrunken and blemished, but it penetrates into mortals; he brings external science that serves egoism. That is why selflessness in regard to knowledge is demanded of the esoteric student. Lucifer comes from the old planet; his task on this one is comparable to what the leaven of the old dough means for the new bread. Evil is a good removed from its proper place; what was good on the old planet is no longer so when transferred to ours. The absolute good on one planet brings part of itself as evil to a new planet. Evil is a necessary part of evolution.

One ought not to say that the world is imperfect or incomplete because it contains evil; rather it is complete for that very reason. When a painting depicts wonderful figures of light, together with dark devils, the picture would be spoiled if the devils were removed. The world creator needed evil in order that good could evolve. A good is only good if it has stood the test of evil. For love to reach its highest goal, the love of all, it must pass through the love of self. In *Faust*, Goethe rightly causes Mephistopheles to say: "I am an aspect of the power that always intends evil, and always creates good."

Lecture V

Illness and Death

Berlin, December 13, 1906

Today's subject must obviously concern everyone, for illness and death enters the lives of all; usually it is unbidden and often in a way that is upsetting and even frightening. Death is indeed life's greatest riddle, so much so that the individual who could solve it would have solved also the other great riddle, that of life itself.

It is said that death is a riddle that no one ever has, or ever will solve. People who speak like that have no notion of the arrogance the words imply, nor of the fact that a solution to the riddle does exist, but a solution they fail to understand.

As we are dealing with a far-reaching and important subject, I ask you to bear especially in mind that all we can do is to attempt to answer the specific question, How can illness and death be understood? It is not possible to go into special cases of illness and health; we must confine ourselves to the question of how understanding can be reached concerning these two most important riddles of existence.

The well-known words of Saint Paul: "The wages of sin are death," were for centuries regarded as an answer, a solution to the question concerning death. Nowadays these words have lost their meaning for most educated people. Modern people are unable to see how sin, which belongs to the sphere of morality and is connected with human behavior, can have anything to do with a physical fact such as death. Nor do we see any connection with illness.

Furthermore, the word "sin" is today used in a narrower, more materialistic sense. At the time of Saint Paul, the word was not taken to refer to ordinary failings or shortcomings, nor to anything extreme. The word sin was regarded as being connected with actions done for egoistic or selfish reasons, in contrast to impartial, objective actions. Here we must bear in mind that egoism and selfishness indicate that a person's "I" has reached a stage of independence and self-consciousness. These are aspects that must be taken into account if we are to understand the mind of a spirit such as that of Saint Paul.

Those who wish to reach a deeper understanding of the Old and New Testaments, who strive to grasp their deeper aspects, will be aware of a definite, one might say instinctive, philosophic current that runs through these records. It can be summed up by saying: All living creatures, in all realms of nature, strive towards a particular goal. Those belonging to lower species are still indifferent to pleasure and pain, joy and sorrow, but we find that as life reaches higher levels things change. Those who shudder at the idea of teleology must realize that we are dealing with facts, not putting forward a theory. Every living being, at all levels including that of human beings, strives towards a specific target, a summit for all living creatures: the attainment of individual consciousness.

The initiates from whom the Old and New Testaments

originated looked down to the animal kingdom and saw how all striving is directed towards the eventual attainment of an independent personality endowed with its own inclinations, and its own impulses to action. They also saw that to the independent personality belonged the possibility of egoistic selfish behavior.

A thinker like Paul would say: "If a personality capable of egoistic deeds dwells in a body, then that body is of necessity mortal. A soul possessing independence, self-consciousness, and consequently egoism would never be able to inhabit an immortal body. The two go together: self-conscious personality with one-sidedly developed impulses, and a mortal body. This is what in the Bible is termed "sin," and what Paul defines as: "The wages of sin are death." You will realize that not only this, but also other sayings in the Bible must be modified to be understood. In the course of centuries their meaning has changed, sometimes to the opposite. However, the modification must not alter the original meaning; we must endeavor to transform the meaning given by modern theology into the original one. It will then be discovered that often the issue concerned is not only far more profound than thought at first sight, but also can be readily understood even today. This explanation is necessary in order to see things in the right perspective.

Throughout the ages, thinkers searching for a world conception have concerned themselves with the riddle of death—a riddle to which during thousands of years the most varied solutions have been offered. We cannot go into a historical survey of these solutions; it must suffice to mention just two philosophers, in order to show that contemporary thinkers have nothing substantial to contribute to the issue either.

Take for example a thinker like Schopenhauer. Those

who have read this sentence will be acquainted with his pessimistic outlook: "Life is a disagreeable affair; I shall spend mine pondering it." And they will realize that he could not arrive at any other conclusion than: "Basically death is the consolation for life, and life the consolation for death; for life is miserable; it can be endured only because of the knowledge that death puts an end to it. On the other hand, if one fears death, it is a consolation to know that life is no better, that nothing is lost by dying." That is Schopenhauer's pessimistic view. He makes the Earth-Spirit say: "If new life is continuously to arise, then I need space." At least Schopenhauer was aware that, as life forever brings forth new life, the old must die to provide new space. But as you can see, he provides nothing of significance to the problem of death; what he says elsewhere on the subject only reflects the same view.

In his last book Eduard von Hartmann concerns himself with the riddle of death. He says: "When we consider the most highly evolved being, man, we find that after one or two generations he no longer understands the world. Once a person is old he no longer understands the young. That is why the old must die and the new continuously arrive." Thus, here again, nothing is said that throws light on the riddle of death.

Anthroposophy, or spiritual science, would wish to contribute to present-day world views what it has to say about the cause of illness and death. However, it must first be made clear that, unlike other sciences, spiritual science cannot speak in such an easy manner; it cannot treat every subject alike. Today's natural scientists do not understand that when illness and death are considered, a distinction must be made between humans and animals. In fact, if today's lecture is to be comprehensible, we must restrict it to that which applies to humans. Few of the things said today will apply to either the animal or vegetable kingdom. This is because the beings of the various kingdoms do not have certain abstract similarities; each kingdom has its own specific characteristic. In the main we shall speak only of human beings; anything else will be brought up merely for the sake of clarification.

For an understanding of illness and death in relation to human beings, it is important to bear in mind that, as spiritual science explains, a person is an extremely complex being. An individual's nature can only be understood on the basis of these following four members: first, the externally visible, physical body; second, the ether or life body; third, the astral body; and fourth, the "I," or the center of the being. We must recognize that the forces and substances of the physical body are the same as those found in the physical world outside, and further that the ether body, which we have in common with the vegetable kingdom, contains the forces that call the physical substances to life. The astral body, which we have in common with the animal kingdom, is the bearer of the life of feelings, craving, pleasure and pain, joys and sorrows. The "I" makes human beings the crown of creation, for that an individual alone possesses.

When we consider a person's physical organism, we must be aware of the fact that within it the other three members are at work; they are the architects and contain the formative forces. The physical principle works on the physical organism, but only up to a point; in certain areas it is mainly the ether body that is at work, in others the astral body, and in yet others the "I." From the viewpoint of spiritual science, the physical human being proper consists of bones and muscles, that is, of those organs that support and make him a firm structure so that he can walk about on the earth. It is, strictly speaking, only these organs that come into being wholly through the physical principle. However, to them must be added the organs that are comparable to physical instruments—the senses. The eye functions like a camera obscura, the ear like a complex musical instrument. What is significant is that these organs are built up by the first principle, whereas all the organs connected with growth, propagation and digestion are built not only by the physical principle, but also by the ether or life body.

Only the organs built according to physical laws are sustained by the physical principle; the processes of digestion, propagation and growth are sustained by the etheric principle. The astral body is the creator of the whole nervous system, right up to the brain, and also of the spinal cord and nerve fibers. Finally, the "I" is the architect of the blood circulation. In contemplating the human organism from the spiritual-scientific viewpoint, you will realize that the four members are in reality four entities that are completely different from one another. These entities have merged, and work together within human beings right down into the externally visible aspect of a person's organism. The four members of a person's being have different values. We shall understand their significance when we investigate how human development is dependent upon each of them.

Today we shall speak, mainly from the physiological viewpoint, about the work the physical principle accomplishes on a person's organism between birth and the change of teeth. During this period, the physical principle works on the physical body, just as before birth the forces and substances of the maternal organism work on the embryo. From the age of seven till puberty it is mainly the etheric principle that works on the physical body; after puberty it is mainly the forces of the astral body that are at work. Thus, we must think of the human embryo being enveloped by the maternal body up to the moment of birth; at that point the maternal body is, as it were, pushed aside; the senses are freed; the outer world begins to influence the human organism. Then at the age of seven another enveloping sheath is pushed aside. The development of an individual's being can only be understood when we recognize that at the change of teeth something happens spiritually that is similar to what happens physically at birth. The human being is truly born a second time about the seventh year, for the ether body is born and can begin to work independently, just as was the case with the physical body at its birth. The maternal body acts physically on the embryo before birth; up to the change of teeth the spiritual forces of the ether world act on the human ether body. At about the seventh year they are pushed aside, as was the maternal body at physical birth. Up to the seventh year the ether body remains latent within the physical body. At the time of the change of teeth the situation in regard to the ether body is comparable to a piece of wood being ignited. Up till then it was tied to the physical body; now it is freed and can act independently. The ether body's release is announced by the change of teeth. Those with deeper insight into human development recognize that the change of teeth is a significant event. Up to the age of seven the physical principle is at work unfettered, while the etheric and astral principles are still latent, that is, not yet born from their spiritual sheaths.

Up to the age of seven the human being displays a number of inherited factors. These are not built up by his own principles, but are derived from ancestors. The milk teeth belong to this category. Only the second teeth are produced by the child's own physical principle, whose particular task is to build up what constitutes the body's firm support. Before the physical principle produces the second teeth, which are the hardest part of the body's supporting structure and the culmination of its work — it works within the bodily nature, while the ether body, the principle of growth, is still latent.

Once the physical principle has finished its work, the ether body is freed and works on the physical organs up to puberty. At this time another covering, the external astral sheath, is thrust aside as was the maternal body at physical birth. Thus, at puberty the human being is born for the third time when the astral body is freed. At this stage the forces of the ether body culminate their creative activity by producing sexual maturity in the organs connected with propagation. In the seventh year the physical principle culminates its activity by producing the teeth as the last hard structure, and in the ether body the principle of growth is freed. Correspondingly, the moment the astral principle is freed, it produces the greatest concentration of urges and cravings, that is, expression of life insofar as it is bound up with the physical nature. As the physical principle is concentrated in the formation of the second teeth, so is the principle of growth concentrated in bringing about sexual maturity. This sets free the astral body, the sheath of the "I," which then begins its work on the astral body.

A cultivated person does not follow his urges and passions blindly; he has purified and transformed them into moral feelings and ethical ideals. When we compare a person with a savage, we realize that a Johann von Schiller,[1] a Francis of Assisi[2] or indeed the average civilized person has purified and transformed, through his "I," these urges and cravings. Consequently the

82

astral body consists of two parts, one that contains the original tendencies and another created by the "I." We can only understand the work of the "I" on the basis of reincarnation; we must recognize that we are subject to repeated lives on earth, which means that when we are born we bring with ourselves the fruits, the outcome of earlier lives. These fruits are contained in four separate bodies as the measure of energy and forces available to a person in life. Thanks to what a person has attained already, one person will be born with strong energy and forces with which to work on the astral body, while another will soon exhaust what is available to him.

By investigating clairvoyantly how the "I" spontaneously begins to work on the astral body, controlling urges and cravings, and by estimating the measure of energy the "I" has brought with it, it is possible to say for how long the "I" will be able to carry out its work. After puberty, every human being has available a measure of energy according to which one can estimate when he will have transformed in his astral body all that is possible for him in this life. The life force a person manages to purify and transform in his inner nature sustains itself. As long as it lasts, a person exists at the expense of what is self-sustaining in the astral body. Once it is exhausted, an individual loses the inclination to transform his cravings further; in short, a person lacks the energy to work on the self. This is when the thread of life begins to wear out, as of necessity it must in proportion to the measure allotted each human being. It is the time when the astral body must derive its forces from the principle of life that is nearest, that is, from the ether body. The astral body now lives at the expense of the forces stored in the ether body. This comes to expression as a gradual loss of memory and creative imagination.

That the ether body is the bearer of creative imagination and memory, and also of everything that can be termed fortitude and confidence in life, has often been explained. When these things attain a permanent character, they become a feature of the ether body. But they are drawn out by the astral body now that it exists at the expense of the ether body. When everything the ether body can give is exhausted, the astral body begins to consume the creative forces of the physical body. When these are used up, the life of the physical body dwindles, the body hardens, and the pulse slows down. Thus, at the end, the astral body lives at the expense of the physical body, depriving it of its forces. It can no longer be maintained by the physical principle.

If the astral body is to become free so that it can emerge and participate in the life and work of the "I," it must, when its allotted task is over in the later part of life, necessarily consume the sheaths it built up. Thus, is individual life created out of the "I."

What takes place can be compared with what happens when a piece of wood is set alight. Wood could not give birth to fire if it were differently constituted. A flame leaps from the wood, consuming it. The nature of the flame is to free itself and in so doing consume the foundation that gave it existence. The astral body is born three times in this way, each time consuming its own foundation as the flame consumes the wood. What gives individual life the possibility of existence is the fact that it absorbs its own foundation. The root of individual life is death; no individual conscious life could exist if there were no death. Death can only be understood by seeking and recognizing its origin; and life by recognizing its relation to death. The origin of illness can be discovered through a similar approach, which will also throw more light on that of death. Every illness destroys life to some degree. But what exactly is illness?

To understand illness we must look at the way human beings are related to the surrounding world of nature. Let us look at what takes place between a person as a living being and the rest of the natural world. With every breath, sound, light, and morsel of food that a person absorbs, he enters into a reciprocal relationship with nature. If you look at the matter more closely, you will realize, even without spiritual sight, that what exists in the outer world actually builds up the physical organs and causes the senses to function. When certain animals wandered into caves and stayed there, their eyes in time atrophied. The eye, a sense predisposed to light, cannot exist without light; conversely, only where there is light can this sense develop. Hence Goethe could say that the eye is created by the light, for the light. Naturally, the physical body is built up according to what might be designated as the inner architect, but the external substances are the material this architect uses.

Once this is fully recognized, we see the various forces and substances in a different light in relation to human beings. The genuine mystic, with his deeper insight, can tell us much in this respect. Paracelsus,[3] for example, saw the whole external world as an extended human organism, and a person's being as an extract of that world. According to Paracelsus, one can say, when looking at a plant: This plant is composed according to certain laws; in a person's healthy or sick organism something exists to which the plant corresponds. Thus, Paracelsus calls a patient suffering from cholera an "arsenicus," because he saw arsenic as the remedy for cholera. There exists in nature something that relates to every human organ. If we could extract an essence of the whole natural world and give it human form, the result would be a human being. The letters that spell

MAN are, as it were, spread throughout the whole of nature. This indicates how nature acts upon a human being and why he must construct his being from the materials of nature. Basically, everything absorbed by our life processes to build up the organism originated in external nature. When we understand the secret of how the external forces and substances are called to life, we shall also understand illness.

Nowadays the educated person finds difficulty in recognizing that many modern ideas concerned with medicine are extremely vague. If someone with knowledge of natural remedies mentions the word "poison," it immediately stirs up all kinds of suppositions. But what is a poison? What is an abnormal effect on the human organism? Whatever is introduced into the human organism acts according to natural laws; that anyone should think it could act otherwise is incomprehensible. But what is a poison? Water, if taken by the bucketful all at once, is a strong poison. What is today looked upon as poison could have most beneficial effects if rightly administered. It always depends on the quantity and the circumstances under which a substance is administered. Nothing, as such, is a poison.

A tribe in Africa uses a certain species of dog for hunting; in the same region there is a fly whose venom is deadly to the dogs they sting. The savages living by the Sambesi River have found a remedy for these stings. They take the bitches in pup to an area where there is an abundance of tsetse flies and let them be bitten. The tribe knows how to arrange matters so that the bitches do not die before the pups arrive. The pups born in this way are immune to the tsetse fly's sting and can be used for hunting.

This illustrates an important fact for understanding the element of life. When a poison is taken up into the process of life, just where a descending line passes over into an ascending one, the poison becomes an integral part of the organism. What is absorbed in this way not only strengthens but protects the organism.

Spiritual investigation shows that such a process is involved in the building up of the human organism. If you like, we might express it by saying that pure substances, which were originally poisonous, form the human organism; today's foodstuff can be absorbed because, through recurrent processes similar to the one described, we have become immune to their harmful effects. The more of such substances we have incorporated, the stronger we are. Rejecting external substances only makes us weak.

In regions where medicine is still based on occult knowledge, the healer even enlists his own body in the quest for remedies. For example, there are cures where he administers to himself the venom of a certain species of snake, in order to make his saliva into a remedy against their bite. He incorporates the poison into his own organism, thus making himself the bearer of healing forces. He becomes strong himself and makes others strong to withstand that particular venom.

The organism must necessarily incorporate what is outside in nature. All the harmless substances contained in the body have become so through the process indicated. However, as human beings are continuously exposed to substances that could become harmful, the possibility always exists that their effects go beyond the limit, and danger arises. This will depend upon whether the ether body is capable of absorbing the substance or not. If the organism is strong enough to absorb such a substance immediately, its tolerance greatly increases. We cannot avoid illness if we wish to be healthy. The possibility to gain sufficient strength to withstand harmful influences depends upon our capacity to become ill. Thus, health is conditioned by illness. The outcome, the gift bestowed upon us by illness, is greater strength. When the illness is overcome, the fruit of the experience is immunity to the illness, and this is retained even after death.

Whoever ponders these things will gain an understanding of illness and death. If we wish to have strength and health, we must accept into the bargain the preliminary condition of illness. To attain strength we must absorb weakness and transform it into strength. If this is grasped in a living way, illness and death become comprehensible. It is this comprehension spiritual science wishes to bring to humanity. Many will see it as something that speaks only to the intellect, but if the intellect has once fully grasped all that is implied, it will bring about an inner mood of deep accord. Comprehension of these things becomes wisdom of life.

You may well have heard it said that anthroposophical truths, derived as they are from spiritual knowledge, can be dangerous! We have plenty of opponents who maintain that anthroposophy is a poison and is harmful. Well, anthroposophists and esotericists themselves know that anthroposophy can be harmful because, in order to make human beings strong, it must be absorbed and digested. Anthroposophy is not something one can argue about; it acts as a spiritual power of healing, and its truths will be confirmed by life itself.

Spiritual science knows that the spirit creates the physical; therefore, when spiritual forces work upon the ether body, they have a health-giving effect also on the physical body. If our concepts and ideas about the world and life are sound, these healthy thoughts will act as a powerful force of heeling. Anthroposophical truths can be harmful only to natures made weak by materialism and naturalism; when they can be absorbed and digested they make a person strong. Only when that happens can anthroposophy fulfill its task.

Goethe answered the question concerning life and death beautifully when he said: "Everything in nature is life; she only invented death to have more life." One could add that, as well as death, nature also invented illness in order to produce strong health. Furthermore, she had to endow wisdom with apparently harmful effects to make it a powerful force of healing.

The anthroposophical world movement differs from other movements that may provide logical proofs to be argued and debated. Anthroposophy does not wish to be something that can be proved simply through logical arguments. It wishes to provide both spiritual and bodily health. Living proof of its truth will be increasingly discovered the more it is seen to enhance life, transforming discontentment into contentment. Spiritual science is like the so-called poison which, when transformed, fructifies life and becomes a source of healing.

Lecture VI

Education in the Light of Spiritual Science

Cologne, December 1, 1906

When the spiritual scientific movement began its activity some thirty years ago, its aim was not to satisfy curiosity about the spiritual worlds, but to make spiritual knowledge available to a wider public, and provide insight that will help to solve not only spiritual but also everyday practical problems. One such problem is the subject of today's lecture. It belongs to everyday life and must be of interest to everyone. Knowledge of human nature and problems of education are intimately connected. No aspect of social life can benefit more from spiritual research than education, because it is possible to provide practical guidelines in this realm through supersensible knowledge.

In order to deal with this subject we must look once more at the nature of human beings. That aspect of their being that is grasped by the intellect is for spiritual science only part of their nature. The physical, bodily aspect that we can see and touch a person has in common with the rest of the natural world. The spiritual investigator's research is not based on speculation, but on what is discovered through the higher sense of clairvoyant sight. This reveals the ether body as the second member of a person's being. It is a spiritual organism that is considerably more delicate and refined than the physical body. It has nothing to do with physical ether, and is best described as a sum of forces or currents of energy rather than as substance.

The ether body is the architect of the physical body. The latter has crystallized out of the ether body much as ice crystallizes out of water. We must therefore regard everything that constitutes the physical aspect of a person's being as having evolved out of the ether body. Human being's have this member in common with all beings endowed with life, that is, with the vegetable and animal kingdoms. In shape and size the ether body coincides with the physical body except for the lower part, which differs in shape from the physical. In animals the ether body extends far beyond the physical. For someone who has developed the spiritual faculties that slumber in every human being, there is nothing fantastic about this description of the ether body, just as it is not fantastic for a person who can see to describe colors to a blind person as blue or red.

The third member of a person's being, the astral body, is the bearer of all kinds of passions, lower as well as higher, and also of joys and sorrows, pleasure and pain, cravings and desires. Our ordinary thoughts and will-impulses are also contained in the astral body. Like the ether body, it becomes visible when the higher senses are developed. The astral body permeates the physical and ether bodies and surrounds humans like a kind of cloud. We have it in common with the animal kingdom; it is in continuous movement, mirroring every shade of feeling. But why the name "astral?"

The physical substances of which the physical body is composed connect it with the whole earth; in like manner is the astral body connected with the world of stars. The forces that permeate it and condition a person's destiny and character were given the name "astral" by those who were able to look deeply into their mysterious connection with the astral world that surrounds the earth.

The fourth member of a person's being, the power that enables him or her to say "I," makes the human being the crown of creation. This name can only be applied to himself; it expresses the fact that what speaks is the soul's primordial divine spark. The designations of everything else we share with others; they can reach a person's ear from outside, but not the name that refers to what is god-like in each individual human soul. That is why in Hebrew esoteric schools it was called the "inexpressible name of God—Jahve," the "I am the I am." Even the priest could utter it only with a shudder. This "I am the I am" the soul ascribes to itself.

The human physical body is related to the mineral kingdom, the ether body to the vegetable kingdom and the astral body to the animal kingdom. The "I" humans have in common with no other earthly being; the "I" makes a person the crown of creation. This fourfold entity has always been known in esoteric schools as the "quaternity of man's nature."

These four bodies develop in each individual in a particular way from childhood till old age. That is why, if we are to understand a person, we must always consider each human being individually. A person's characteristics are indicated already in the embryo. However, humans are not isolated beings; they develop within a certain environment, and can thrive only when surrounded by all the beings of the universe. During embryonic life they must be enveloped by the maternal organism, from which they become independent only when a certain stage of maturity is reached. During further development, the child goes through more events of a similar nature. Just as the physical body while still at the embryonic stage must be enveloped by the maternal organism, so is it surrounded after birth by spiritual sheaths related to spiritual realms. The child is enveloped by an etheric and an astral sheath; the child reposes in them as he did in the womb before birth.

At the time of the change of teeth an etheric covering loosens itself from the ether body, as did the physical covering at physical birth. That means that the ether body is born and becomes free in all directions. Up to then an entity of like nature to itself was attached to it, from which spiritual currents flowed through it as physical currents flowed from the maternal covering through the child before birth. Thus, the child is born for a second time when the ether body is born. Meanwhile the astral body is still surrounded by its protective sheath, a covering that strengthens and invigorates it up to the time of puberty. Then that too withdraws; the birth of the astral body takes place; and the child is born for the third time.

The fact that a threefold birth takes place indicates that the three entities must be considered separately. While it is impossible for external light to reach and harm the eyes of the unborn child, it is not impossible, but certainly highly damaging to the soul, if influences foreign to it are brought to bear on the ether body before it has become completely independent. The same applies to the astral body before puberty. We should, according to spiritual science, avoid all education and training before the change of teeth, except such that have a bearing on the child's physical body; we should in fact influence the ether body as little as we influence the child's physical body before it is born. However, just as the mother must be cared for, because her health influences the development of the embryo, so one should now respect the inviolability of the ether body for the sake of the child's healthy development. This is so important because before the change of teeth only the physical body is ready to be influenced by the external world; all training should therefore be restricted to what concerns the physical body. Any external influence of the ether body during this period is a violation of laws according to which human beings develop.

The human ether body is different from that of the plant world because in a person it becomes the bearer of his enduring traits such as habit, character, conscience and memory, and also temperament. The astral body is the seat of the life of feelings already mentioned, and also of the ability to discern, to judge.

These facts indicate when it becomes right to exert influence on the natural tendencies. In the period up to the seventh year, the child's bodily faculties develop; they become independent and self-contained. The same applies between the seventh and the fourteenth years to habits, memory, temperament and so on; between the fourteenth and the twentieth or twenty-second years is the time when the faculty of the critical intellect develops, and an independent relation to the surrounding world is attained. All these things indicate that different principles of education are required in the various life periods. Special care must be taken up to the seventh year with everything that affects the physical body. This encompasses a great many things. It is a time when all the essential physical organs are gradually developing and the effect on the child's senses is of immense importance. It matters greatly what it sees and hears and generally absorbs. The faculty most prominent at this time is imitation. The Greek philosopher Aristotle[1] remarked that human beings are the most imitative of all animals. This is especially true of the child before the change of teeth. Everything is imitated during this time, and as whatever enters the child through its senses as light and sound works formatively on the organs, it is of utmost importance that what surrounds the child should act beneficially.

At this age nothing is achieved by admonition; commands and prohibitions have no effect whatever. But of the greatest significance is the *example*. What the child sees, what happens around him, he feels must be imitated. For instance: the parents of a well-behaved child were astonished to discover that he had taken money from a cashbox; greatly disturbed, they thought the child had inclinations to steal. Questioning brought to light that the child had simply imitated what he had seen his parents do every day.

It is important that the examples the child sees and imitates are of a kind thatawaken its inner forces. Exhortations have no effect, but the way a person behaves in the child's presence matters greatly. It is far more important to refrain from doing what the child is not permitted to do than to forbid the child to imitate it.

Thus, it is vital that during these years the educator is an exemplary example, that he or she only does what is worthy of imitation. Education should consist of example and imitation. The truth of this is recognized when insight is attained into the nature of human beings and confirmed by the results of education based upon it. Thus, because the ability to understand what things *mean* is a faculty of the ether body, the child should not learn the significance of the letters of the alphabet before the change of teeth; before then, he or she should do no more than trace their form with paint.

Spiritual research makes all these subtleties under-standable and throws light even on details of what should be done. Everything the child perceives, also in a moral sense, acts on the formation of its physical organs. It makes a difference whether the child is surrounded by pain and sorrow or happiness and joy. Happiness and joy build sound organs, and lay the foundation for future health. The opposite can create a disposition towards illness. Everything that surrounds the child should breathe an atmosphere of happiness and joy, even down to objects and colors of clothing and wallpaper. The educator must ensure that it does so, while also taking into account the child's particular disposition.

If a child is inclined to be too earnest and too quiet, it will benefit from having in its surroundings rather sombre, bluish, greenish colors, while the lively, too active child should have yellow, reddish colors. This may seem like a contradiction, but the fact is that through its inherent nature the sense of sight calls up the opposite colors. The bluish shades have an invigo-rating effect, while in the lively child the yellow-reddish shades call up the opposite colors.

Thus, you see that spiritual investigation throws light even on practical details. The developing organs must be treated in ways that promote their health and inner forces. The child should not be given toys that are too finished and perfect, such as building blocks or perfect dolls. A doll made out of an old table napkin on which eyes, nose and mouth are indicated is far better. Every child will see such a homemade doll as a lady attired in beautiful finery. Why? Because it stirs its imagination, and that induces movement in the inner organs and produces in the child a feeling of well-being. Notice in what a lively and interested manner such a child plays, throwing itself body and soul into what the imagination conjures up, while the child with the perfect doll just sits, unexcited and unamused. It has no possibility to add anything through imagination, so its inner organs are condemned to remain inactive. The child has an extraordinarily sound instinct for what is good for it, as long as only the physical body has become free to interact with the external world, and as long as it is in the process of development. The child will indicate what is beneficial for himself. However, if from early on this instinct is disregarded, it will disappear. Education should be based on happiness, on joy and the child's natural cravings. To practice asceticism at this age would be synonymous with undermining its healthy development.

When the child approaches the seventh year and the milk teeth are gradually being replaced, the covering of the ether body loosens and it becomes free, as did the physical body at physical birth. Now the educator must bring to bear everything that will further the development of the ether body. However, the teacher must guard against placing too much emphasis on developing the child's reason and intellect. Between the seventh and twelfth years, it is mainly a question of authority, confidence, trust and reverence. Character and habit are special qualities of the ether body and must be fostered; but it is harmful to exert any influence on the reasoning faculty before puberty.

The development of the ether body occurs in the period from the seventh to the sixteenth year (in girls to the fourteenth). It is important for the rest of a person's life that during this period feelings of respect and veneration are fostered. Such feelings can be awakened in the following way: by means of information and narration, the lives of significant people are depicted to the child, not only from history, but from the child's own circle, perhaps that of a revered relative. Awe and reverence are awakened in the child, which forbid him to harbor any critical thoughts or opposition against the venerated person. The child lives in solemn expectation of the moment he will be permitted to meet this person. At last the day arrives and the child stands before the door filled with awe and veneration; he turns the handle, enters the room that for him, is a holy place. Such moments of veneration become forces of strength in later life. It is immensely important that the educator, the teacher, is at this time a respected authority for the child. A child's faith and confidence must be awakened, not in axioms, but in human beings.

People around the child with whom he has contact must be his ideals; the child must also choose such ideals from history and literature: "Everyone must choose the hero whose path to Olympus he will follow," is a true saying. The materialistic view that opposes authority and undervalues respect and reverence is utterly wrong. It regards the child as being already self-reliant, but its healthy development is impaired if demands are made upon the reasoning faculty before the astral body is born. What *is* important at this time is that memory is developed. This is best done in purely mechanical fashion. However, calculators should not be used; tables of multiplication, poems and so on should be committed to memory in quite a parrot fashion. It is simply materialistic prejudice that maintains that at this age such things should be inwardly felt and understood.

In the old days educators knew better. At the ages between one and seven all kinds of songs were sung to the children, like the good old nursery rhymes and children's songs. What mattered was not sense and meaning but sound; the children were made aware of harmony and consonance; we often find words inserted purely for the sake of their sound. Often the rhymes were meaningless. For example: "Fly beetle fly, your father is away; your mother is in Pommerland, Pommerland, fly beetle fly." Incidentally, in the idiom of children "Pommerland" meant motherland. The expression stemmed from a time when it was still believed that human beings were spiritual beings and had come down to earth from a spiritual world. Pommerland was the land of spiritual origin. Yet it was not the meaning in such rhymes that was important, but the sound; hence, the many children's songs had no particular sense.

This is the age when memory, habit and character must be established, and this is achieved through authority. If the foundation of these traits is not laid during this period, it will result in behavioral shortcomings later. Just because axioms and rules of conduct have no place in education until the astral body is born, it is important that the prepuberty child, if he is to be properly educated, can look up to authority. The child is able to sense a person's innermost being, and that is what it reveres in those with authority. Whatever flows from the educator to the child forms and develops conscience, character and even the temperament—its lasting disposition. During these years allegories and symbols act formatively on the ether body of the child because they make manifest the world-spirit. Fairy tales, legends and descriptions of heroes are a true blessing.

During this period, the ether body must receive as much care as the physical body. During the earlier period it was happiness and joy that influenced the forming of the organs; from seven to fourteen (in this case boys to sixteen), the emphasis must be on everything that promotes feelings of health and vigor. Hence, the value of gymnastics. However, the desired effect will not be attained if the instructor aims at movements that solely benefit the physical body. It is important that the teacher be able to intuitively enter into how the child inwardly senses himself, and in this way to know which movements will promote inner sensations of health, strength, well-being, and pleasure in the bodily constitution. Only when gymnastic exercises induce feelings of growing strength are they of real value. Not only the external aspect of the bodily nature benefits from correct gymnastic exercises, but also the way a person inwardly experiences the self.

Everything artistic has a strong influence on the ether, as well as the astral body. Music of excellence, both vocal and instrumental, is particularly important, especially for the ether body. And there should be many objects of true artistic beauty in the child's environment.

Most important of all is religious instruction. Images of things supersensible are deeply imprinted in the ether body. What is important here is not the pupil's ability to have an opinion about religious faith, but that he receives descriptions of the supersensible, of what extends beyond the temporal. All religious subjects must be presented pictorially.

Great care must be taken that what is taught is brought to life. Much is spoiled in the child if it is burdened with too much that is dull and lifeless. What is taught in a lively interesting manner benefits the child's ether body. There should be much activity and doing; this has a quickening effect on the spirit. That is true also when it comes to play. The old kind of picture books have a stimulating effect because they contain figures that can be pulled by strings and suggest movement and inner life. Nothing has a more deadening effect on the child's spirit than putting together and fixing some structure, using finished geometrical shapes. That is why building blocks should not be used; the child should create everything from the beginning and learn to bring to life what he forms out of the lifeless. Our materialistic age extinguishes life through mass-produced lifeless objects. Much dies in the young developing brain when the child has to do meaningless things like, for example, braiding. Talents are stifled and much that is unhealthy in our modern society can be traced back to the nursery. Inartistic lifeless toys do not foster trust in spiritual life. A fundamental connection exists between today's lack of religious belief and the way young children are taught.

Once puberty is reached, the astral covering falls away; the astral body becomes independent. With the awakening feelings for the opposite sex, the ability to judge, to form personal opinion, also awakens. Only now should appeal be made to the reasoning faculty, to the approval or disapproval of the critical intellect. That is not to say that the moment the human being has reached this age he is capable of forming independent judgment, let alone do so earlier. It is absurd for such young people to judge issues or to have a say in cultural life. A young person under the age of twenty has an as yet undeveloped astral body, and can no more make sound judgments than a baby still in the womb can hear or see. Each life period requires a corresponding influence. In the first, it is a model to imitate; in the second an authority to emulate; the third requires rules of conduct, principles, and axioms. What is of utmost significance for the young person at this time is the *teacher*, the *personality* that will guide the student's eagerness for learning and his desire for independence in the right directions.

Thus, the spiritual scientific world conception provides an abundance of basic principles that help the teacher's task of developing and educating the young generations. We have shown that spiritual science is applicable to everyday life and capable of practical intervention in important issues. We must understand all the members of the human being, and the way they are interrelated in order to know when to influence which member in a truly beneficial way. The embryo will be affected if the expectant mother is not properly nourished; for its sake the mother must be cared for. Similarly, what later still surrounds and protects the child must also be cared for, as that in turn will benefit the child. This holds good on both physical and spiritual levels. Thus, as long as the child still slumbers as if within an etheric womb and is still rooted in the astral covering, it matters greatly what happens in the environment. The child is affected by every thought, every feeling, every sentiment motivating those around him, even if not expressed. Here a person cannot maintain that one's thoughts and feelings do not matter as long as nothing is said.

Even in the innermost recesses of their hearts, those around the child cannot permit themselves ignoble thoughts or feelings. Words affect only the external senses, whereas thoughts and feelings reach the protecting sheaths of the ether and astral bodies and pass over to the child. Therefore, as long as these protective coverings envelop the child, they must be cared for. Impure thoughts and passions harm them just as unsuitable substances harm the mother's body.

Thus, even subtle aspects are illumined by spiritual science. Through knowledge of the human being the educator gains the insight needed. Spiritual science does not aim to persuade; it is not a theory, it is practical knowledge applicable to life. Its effect is beneficial, for it makes human beings healthier both physically and spiritually. It provides effective truth that must flow into every aspect of life. There is no better way for spiritual science to serve humanity than fostering social impulses in the young during the formative years. What takes place in human beings during the time they grow up and mature is one of life's greatest riddles; those who find practical solutions will prove true educators.

Lecture VII

Education and Spiritual Science

Berlin, January 24, 1907

When we discuss subjects such as that of today's lecture, we must keep before our mind's eye mankind's whole evolution. Only then can we understand the evolution of the individual, and guide the young through education. At the center of education is the school. We shall attempt to understand what is required of education on the basis of human nature and a person's evolution in general.

We see a person's being as consisting of four distinct members: physical body, ether or life body, astral body, and at the center of the being, the "I." When an individual is born, only the physical body is ready to receive influences from the external world. Not until the time of the change of teeth is the ether body born, the astral body not until puberty is reached. The faculties of the ether body, such as memory, temperament, and so on, are, up to the change of teeth, protected by an etheric sheath, just as the physical senses of eyes and ears are protected before physical birth by the material body. The educator must during this time leave undisturbed what should develop naturally of itself.

Jean Paul expressed it by saying that no world traveller learns as much on his far-flung journeys as the little child learns from his nurse before the age of seven. Why then must we have schools for children?

What only evolves after the physical birth has taken place is in need of a protective covering just as the embryo needs the protection of the maternal body. Not until a certain stage of development is reached does the human being begin a life that is entirely new. Up to then his life is a repetition of earlier epochs. Even the embryo repeats all primordial stages of evolution up to the present. And after birth, the child repeats earlier human evolutionary epochs.

Friedrich August Wolf [1] describes the stages through which a human being evolves from childhood onwards as follows: The first epoch, lasting up to the third year, he calls the "golden, gentle, harmonious age" corresponding to the life of today's Indian and South Sea Islander. The second epoch, up to the sixth year, reflects the Asiatic wars and their repercussions in Europe, and also the Greek heroic age, as well as the time of the North American savage. The third epoch, up to the ninth year, corresponds to the time from Homer [2] to Alexander the Great. [3] The fourth epoch, up to the twelfth year, corresponds to the time of the Roman Empire. The fifth epoch, up to the fifteenth year, when the inner forces should be ennobled through religion, corresponds to the Middle Ages. The sixth epoch, up to the eighteenth year, corresponds to the Renaissance. The seventh epoch, up to the twenty-first year, corresponds to the Reformation, and in the eighth epoch, lasting up to the twenty-fourth year, a human reaches the present.

This system is on the whole a valuable spiritual foundation, but it must be widened considerably to correspond to reality. It must include the whole of a human being's evolutionary descent. A person does not stem from the animal kingdom, though certainly from beings who, in regard to physical development, were far below what human beings are today. Yet in no way did they resemble apes.

Spiritual science points back to a time when human beings inhabited Atlantis;[4] compared with modern human beings the Atlantean's soul and spirit were differently constituted. Their consciousness could be termed somnambulistic; the intellect was undeveloped— they could neither count nor write, and logical reasoning did not exist. But they beheld many aspects of the spiritual world. The will that flowed through their limbs was immensely strong. The higher animals such as apes were degenerate descendants of the Atlanteans.

Our dream consciousness is a residue of the Atlantean's normal pictorial consciousness, which could be compared with that of a person experiencing vivid dreams during sleep. But the pictures of the Atlantean were animated, more vivid than those of today's most fertile imagination. Furthermore, an Atlantean was able to control his pictures, which were not chaotic. We see an echo of this consciousness when young children play, investing their toys with pictorial content.

The human being first descended into physical bodies during Lemurian time. A person repeats that event during physical birth. At that time, having descended into a physical body, a person begins developing through soul and spirit to ever higher levels. The Lemurian and Atlantean epochs are repeated in a child's development up to the seventh year. Between the change of teeth and puberty that epoch of evolution is repeated in which great spiritual teachers have appeared among men. Buddha,[5] Plato,[6] Pythagoras,[7]

Hermes,[8] Moses,[9] and Zarathustra[10] are some of the latter. In those days, the influence of the spiritual world was much greater, a fact we find preserved in heroic legends and sagas. It is therefore important that what is taught during this period of the child's life conveys the spirit of the earlier cultural epochs.

The period between the seventh and fourteenth years corresponds in the child to the time up to the twelfth century, the time when cities were founded. The main emphasis must now be on authority and community. The children should experience something of the power and glory that surrounded the early leaders. The most important issue that concerns a school is therefore the teacher. The teacher's authority must be self-evident for the children, just as what was taught by the great teachers was self-evident to the human soul. It is bad; it does great harm if the child doubts the teacher. The child's respect and reverence must be without reservation, so that the teacher's kindness and good will—which he naturally must have—seem to the child like a blessing. What is important is not pedagogical methods and principles, but the teacher's profound psychological insight. The study of psychology is the most important subject of a teacher's training. An educator should not be concerned with how the human being ought to develop, but with the reality of how the student in fact does develop.

As every age makes different demands, it is useless to lay down general rules. It is not knowledge or proficiency in pedagogical methods that matter in a teacher, but character and a certain presence that makes itself felt even before the teacher has spoken. The educator must have attained a degree of inner development, and must have become not merely learned, but inwardly transformed. The day will come when a teacher will be tested, not for knowledge or even for pedagogical principles, but for what he or she is as a human being.

For the child the school must be its life. Life should not just be portrayed; former epochs must come to life. The school must create a life of its own, not draw it from outside. What the human being will no longer be able to receive later in life he must receive at school. Pictorial and symbolic concepts must be fostered. The teacher must be deeply aware of the truth that: "Everything transient is but a semblance." When the educator presents a subject pictorially the teacher should not be thinking that it is merely allegory. If the teacher fully participates in the life of the child, forces will flow from his or her soul to that of the child. Processes of nature must be described in rich imaginative pictures. The spiritual behind the sense-perceptible must be brought to life. Modern teaching methods fail completely in this respect, because only the external aspects are described. But a seed contains not only the future plant, it contains forces of the sun, indeed of the whole cosmos. A feeling for nature will awaken in the child when the capacity for imagery is fostered. Plants should not merely be shown and described, the child should make paintings of them; then happy human beings for whom life has meaning will emerge from their time at school.

Calculators ought not to be used; one must do sums with the children on living fingers. Vigorous spiritual forces are to be stimulated. Nature study and arithmetic train the power of thinking and memory; history the life of feeling. A sense for what is noble and beautiful awakens love for what is worthy of love. But what strengthens the will is religion; it must permeate every subject that is taught. The child will not immediately grasp everything it is capable of absorbing; this is true of everyone. Jean Paul made the remark that one should listen carefully to the truth uttered by a child, but to have it explained one must turn to its father. In our materialistic age too little is expected of memory. The child first learns; only later does it understand, and only later still will it grasp the underlying laws.

Between the seventh and fourteenth years is also the time to foster the sense for beauty. It is through this sense that we grasp symbolic meaning. But most important is that the child is not burdened with abstract concepts; what is taught should have a direct connection with life. The spirit of nature, in other words the facts themselves existing behind the sense-perceptible, must have spoken to the child; it should have a natural appreciation of things before abstract theories are introduced, which should only be done after puberty. There is no need for concern that things learnt may be forgotten once school days are over; what matters is that what is taught bears fruit and forms the character. What the child has inwardly experienced it will also retain; details may vanish but the essential, the universal, will remain and will grow.

No education can be conducted without a religious foundation; without religion a school is an illusion. Even Haeckel's *Riddle of the Universe* contains religion. No theory can ever replace religion, nor can a history of religion. A person who is basically of a religious disposition, who has deep conviction, will also be able to convey religion. The spirit that lives in the world also lives in humans. The teacher must feel that he or she belongs to a spiritual world-order from which a mission is received.

There is a saying that a person's character is formed partly by study and partly by life. But school and education should not be something apart from life. Rather should it be said that a person's character will be rightly formed when study is also life.

Lecture VIII

Insanity in the Light of Spiritual Science

Berlin, January 31, 1907

Spiritual science more than any other science is in a position to say something about so-called spiritual or mental illness. The name is actually misleading; one cannot speak of the spirit being ill. Furthermore, there is widespread confusion among lay people as well as professionals, mainly because of the way such illnesses are presented in popular literature. The descriptions are thought of as the reality. Megalomania, persecution-mania, religious-mania are spoken of, but these terms only point to symptoms. No one can become insane by being occupied with religious ideas. Yet the most curious statements are put forward, for example that the discord between old and modern world conceptions was the cause of Friedrich Hölderlin's [1] illness. The illness from which he suffered would still have over-taken Holderin even if he had not been a poet; though in that case he would have expressed himself differently.

When a deeply religious person becomes mentally ill, his religious ideas become distorted. Had he been steeped in materialistic ideas, then they would have become distorted. The cause of mental illness is deeply rooted in human nature where it must be sought. All the medical professions can offer in this field are hypotheses, doubt and conjecture. It is indeed difficult from a materialistic viewpoint to come to any conclusive ideas in this realm. Many illnesses that in fact belong in this category are not regarded to do so by the medical profession, for example, querulousness, religious sectarianism and fanaticism. People of the latter kind are possessed by certain hallucinary ideas which, because they have great suggestive power over weaker personalities, can result in veritable epidemics of fanaticism.

The question may be asked: How is it possible for insanity to establish itself in human nature? To answer this question we must turn our attention to the four lower members of a person's being: the physical, etheric and astral bodies, and the "I." The "I" works on the other three members, especially on the astral body, ennobling and purifying it and by compelling it not to follow urges and impulses blindly. The "I" also works on the ether body, particularly through higher impulses, especially of an artistic nature. Under this influence the astral body divides into two parts, one that is purified and one that is not. This occurs also in the ether body, and gradually the purified parts become ever larger. The "I" also works on the physical body, but unconsciously. Only when a high level of initiation is reached can work on the physical be done consciously.

To answer our question, we must also bear in mind the fact of repeated lives. When we go to sleep something takes place that is similar to what occurs at death. When we go to sleep the astral body and the "I" separate from the physical body, and all cravings and sensations sink into dark oblivion. Only the physical and etheric bodies remain on the bed. At death the ether or life body too separates from the physical body, and in the hours that follow, while the human being is still connected with the ether body, there passes, in mighty pictures before the soul, the whole of a person's past life. This lasts until the ether body also separates from that individual and disperses into the general world-ether.

However, only the substance of the ether body separates from the person. Throughout future times an essence, like a memory-picture, remains with the astral body and the "I." These first of all pass over into the condition called "kamaloca" or the region of desire, where everything within the astral body that still clings to earthy life is separated from it. What is not yet ennobled detaches itself; the rest accompanies the soul into the future. This also applies to the physical body, but only to a very slight extent, and only in the case of highly evolved individuals. When the incarnation that will follow draws near, the human being unites once more with what was left behind in order to continue its purification. The more often a human being incarnates, the stronger becomes his character and his moral sense, and the more numerous and greater the talents and abilities.

What we need to bear in mind above all, if we are to understand how insanity arises, is the Hermetic axiom: As above, so below; as below, so above. A smiling face immediately conveys cheerfulness, tears inner sadness. Cheerfulness and sadness we must in this instance see as the "above", and laughter and tears, that is, the material expression of cheerfulness and sadness, as representing the "below." When someone has been rightly brought up and educated, he looks at life with different eyes. To him a flower is seen as the expression of the Earth-Spirit's sadness or cheerfulness. For him this is not just a poetic notion, anymore than the soul is a poetic notion. The spirit of the earth is the foundation of earth existence and is related to it as the above. Everything material is a condensed spirit just as ice is condensed water; as ice can be melted to become water, so can matter be transformed into spirit.

We distinguish in human beings the following physical components that correspond to their higher, that is, their above members: first the purely physical, what is built according to purely physical laws, especially the sense organs. What builds a crystal could also build the human body, though it would be an organism without life. Second, we have everything connected with digestion, growth and propagation built by the ether body; third, the nervous system (brain and spinal cord) built by the astral body; fourth, the blood circulation, of which the "I," living in the blood, is the architect. Thus, we have:

Blood Circulation	I
Nervous System	Astral Body
Propagation	Ether Body
Purely Physical	Physical Body

Everything physical is subject to the laws of physical heredity, but so too are the organs of propagation, the nervous system and the blood circulation. The individuality of a human being must unite with a physical body that is subject to these laws. This means that the "I," together with the ennobled parts of the astral and ether body, and perhaps part of the physical body, must establish harmony between itself and what is inherited. This usually happens through the fact that the spiritual, by transforming itself, adapts to the physical. But what happens when that is not possible, when for example an astral body encounters a nervous system to which it cannot adjust, and therefore cannot make use of?

Delusion caused by visual defect is not regarded as a mental illness. A book by Moritz Benedict,[2] the criminologist and anthropologist, though not written from a spiritual scientific viewpoint, has much of interest to say on this subject. He suffered from a partial cataract in the left eye that impaired his sight. He describes his own experiences: When in the dark he looked in a certain direction and saw spectres of a peculiar kind; he was once so startled that he grabbed a weapon.

The explanation for this kind of phenomenon is as follows: A healthy person is not conscious of the inner constituents of his eye but, if there are irregularities, he becomes aware of them in such a way that they appear as reflected forms, approaching from outside. However, this is something that holds true also for the rest of a person's organism. Normally we are only conscious of what comes to us from outside, not of what goes on inside. When the "above" is in harmony with the "below," one is not at all conscious of inner processes. But, if for instance, the brain is clumsy and sluggish so that the astral body is unable to make use of it, then the astral body suffers disturbance. It projects itself outwardly just as it does when the eye is impaired. It becomes conscious of itself, and feelings of hopes, wishes and cravings, that is, the attributes of the astral body, are projected and appear as forms approaching from outside. Madness, querulousness, hysteria—all conditions in which a person cannot make his feelings agree with what goes on around him—belong to this category. The ether body can also suffer disturbance through inner abnormalities. It contains our mental pictures of the outside world. As long as it is not conscious of itself it receives these pictures in their true form, but if they become projected outwards due to a disturbance of the ether body, the result is delusions and paranoia. When that aspect of the physical body that should bring about the accord with the physical environment becomes disturbed, becomes conscious of itself, it leads to idiocy. A human being can become what is called "demented" when the physical body is too ponderous, too unwieldy, so that the astral body is unable to master it. If on the other hand the physical organs are too mobile so that they fail to express the soul's intentions, the result is paralysis.

A multitude of such cases exist. They may be due to any number of causes. This is true especially of delusions; they can arise from either projections or a sickening of the astral body. The effect may be so strong that delirium sets in; such attacks imprint themselves in the ether body and give rise to delusions. These imprints are like scars from the wounds in the astral body, and are much more difficult to heal than the delirium itself. Glaucoma is often a forerunner of madness.

We must now remind ourselves that human beings go through a threefold birth, first that of the physical body, then at the time of the change of teeth the ether body is born, and at puberty the astral body. It may happen that the disharmony between the "above" and the "below" only becomes noticeable at the time when the astral body is born, because up to that time the astral covering that protected it maintained the harmony. Once it is born the astral body is left to itself, and the discord with the physical body becomes apparent. The form of mental illness that results comes to expression, for the young person suffers from hallucinations, and will often give one and the same answer to a variety of questions. This is called "weak-mindedness or imbecility." It does not come about suddenly, but is gradually prepared from the age of twelve onwards. The preliminary signs are depression, tiredness, argumentativeness, headaches, problems with digestion and with sleep. The condition is extremely difficult to cure; and it is sad that most parents punish their children for such illness, mistaking it for naughtiness.

The spirit itself is always healthy; it cannot be ill, but when it can find no harmony with the "below" it becomes distorted. A face reflected in a convex mirror is distorted, but no one assumes that the real face must therefore also be distorted. The various forms of insanity are the distorted reflections of the spirit in the physical. Consequently, it is quite useless to attempt a cure by means of abstract logical reasoning; such methods have no effect whatever. Nothing is more remote from concentrated spirit than shadowy abstract logic—and our bodily organs *are* concentrated spirit, albeit not *our* spirit—whereas passionate, imaginative, pictorial ideas and images are more akin to spirit, and are capable of driving out the distorted images that cause the condition. Such counter-images must be provided by the strength and power of another personality. An individual cannot through explanations convince the ill person that he is illogical, whereas vivid, strong counter-images will be effective. For example, the power of the other's personality must prove to the sick person that he can, after all, do what he thought was beyond him.

In the realm of so-called spiritual or mental illnesses, natural and spiritual science must work together. What is needed is detailed research so that the counter-images applicable in specific cases are always available. These too are not normal in the usual sense, as they must, to be effective, swing towards the opposite extreme.

117

Spiritual science is neither remote from life nor passive; it aims to contribute to practical life. To be effective in the world one must of necessity learn to understand the spiritual forces that constitute its foundation. If we are to understand the nature of what is physical, we must recognize that the material world is an imprint of the spiritual world. To Hellenbach who says: "What possible concern of ours is all this spirit-rabble?" we must reply: "Well, as human rabble is our concern, and as human beings are connected with the spiritual world, we wish to find the bridge between the two."

Lecture IX

Wisdom and Health

Berlin, February 14, 1907

Spiritual science aims to be an influence in practical life, to be a source of strength and confidence. It is for people who wish to be effective in life, not for the merely curious. Knowledge of the spirit has always existed. It has been fostered in circles where it was recognized that human beings are capable of developing spiritual forces of greater capacity than the ordinary intellect. In these circles there was awareness of the fact that healing was connected with holiness; it was felt that the Holy Spirit was the wholly healthy spirit that united itself with mankind's soul to bring healing to the world.

This aspect is the one least understood. Spiritual knowledge guides the human soul away from narrow attitudes and egoistical aims; it points to universal issues that unite the individual with the cosmos. Nevertheless, the higher forces it bestows often are used as an incentive for egoistical striving. It is often made to serve egoism despite the fact that its very nature is to lead human beings away from the personal; people demand that through spiritual science egoistical wishes should be fulfilled from one day to the next.

There once existed in Africa a brotherhood—the Therapeutae, which fostered spiritual knowledge. In the region where Christianity arose, the same sect was known as the Essenes. The name indicates that the brotherhood was concerned with healing, which they practiced by combining their spiritual insight with knowledge of matter. When spiritual knowledge is absorbed, healing forces are absorbed also. Spiritual science is an elixir of life; though it cannot be proved by argument the proof will be seen when it is assimilated, then applied to life, and health follows.

However, a person might as well know nothing about spiritual science if all that person can do is talk glibly about reincarnation and karma. If its effect is to be experienced, a person's whole inner being must be steeped in spiritual science; one must live it every hour of the day, and calmly be able to wait. In this connection Goethe's saying is apt: "Consider the what, but even more consider the how." Spiritual science is rightly understood if it is assimilated like a spiritual food, and allowed to grow and mature within a person. It is rightly understood if, in moments of sorrow or happiness, of devotion and exaltation, or when life threatens to fall apart, a person experiences the hope, strength and incentive to action it brings.

Spiritual science must become a personal quest. The striving human being, looking at the stars, will recognize the eternal laws that guide them through cosmic space. When clouds sail across the vault of heaven, when the sun rises in splendor, or the moon in silent majesty, a person will see all these phenomena as the expression of soul-spiritual universal life. Just as we recognize the look on a face, or the movement of a hand as the expression of the soul and spirit in human beings, when we look at the past we look at the same time up to the spirit whose imprint in the physical is everywhere in evidence.

Absorb the spirit, and you absorb health-giving forces! Not, however, in lazy comfort; there are people who entertain the most trivial notions while declaring that all one needs is to be in tune with the infinite. That has nothing to do with knowledge of the spirit. Spiritual knowledge must penetrate a human's innermost being. It is not through some magical formula that we discover the spiritual world. What is required is that we enter with patience and love into every being, every event. The spiritual world is there and should not be sought as if it has no connection with the physical. Wherever we find ourselves placed in life, there we must seek it; then spiritual knowledge becomes a personal quest.

There are people who have no sense for music or paintings; likewise there are people with no sense for what is spiritual. The following incident illustrates a common notion of what is spiritual: One evening in a small town, a strange light was noticed to pass across the church wall. Soon it was a topic of conversation all over the town. As no natural explanation was found, it was determined that it was a spiritual phenomenon. Actually, the fact that it was seen by many already made this highly unlikely. If a person was able to perceive a genuine spiritual event, certain spiritual organs and capabilities must first be developed. In our time this is a rare event; so the fact that the strange light was seen by many people is a sure proof that it was not a spiritual manifestation. And indeed an explanation was soon forthcoming: An elderly lady with a lantern was in the habit of walking her dog in the evening. On one particular night the light happened to be noticed. Investigation of such meaningless suppositions was pointless. The most significant spiritual manifestations are to be found in the objects and events around us every day.

Wisdom is science, but also more than science. It is science that is united with, not apart from, reality. At any moment it can become decision and action. Someone who is knowledgeable about scientific laws is a scientist; someone who immediately knows how to apply knowledge so that it becomes reality is wise. Wisdom is science becoming creative. We must so contemplate, so merge with the laws of nature that they become an inner force. Through his contemplation and exact observation of individual plants, Goethe arrived at his inner perception of the archetypal plant. The idea of the archetypal plant is a product of spiritual intuition; it is a plant-image that can come to life within us; from it numberless plants can be derived which do not as yet exist, but could exist. In someone who has become a sage laws are not bound to the particular, they are eternal living entities. This is the realm of Imagination; of ideas that are not abstract but creative images. Abstract concepts and ideas may lead to science, but not to wisdom. Had Goethe remained at the conceptual stage, he would never have discovered the archetypal plant. It must be seen so vividly and so exactly that one can draw it, including root, stem, leaves and fruit, without it resembling any particular plant. Such an image is not a product of fantasy. Fantasy is related to imagination as shadow is to reality; however, it can be transformed and raised to become imagination.

We may not as yet have access to the world of imagination, but it is a world that is attainable.

We must develop soul forces that are objective, comparable to the forces active in our eyes. We would be surrounded by perpetual darkness if the eyes did not transform the light falling upon them into colored images and mental pictures. Anyone who believes we must just wait for some nebulous manifestation of the spirit to appear has no comprehension of the inner work required of human beings. The soul must become active, as the eyes are active transforming light. Unless the soul creates pictures, and images within itself, the spiritual world cannot stream in. The pictures thus created will maintain objectivity provided they are not prompted by egoistic wishes; when their content is spiritual, then healing forces stream into a person's soul. When the ability is attained to transform the concepts of spiritual science into vivid pictures full of color, sound and life; when the whole world becomes such a picture, then this wisdom becomes in all spheres of life a healing force, not only for ourselves, but for others, for the whole world. Even if the pictures we create in the soul are not accurate, it will not matter; they are corrected by that which guides us. Paracelsus was a sage of this kind. He immersed himself in all aspects of nature and transformed his knowledge into vigorous inner forces. Every plant spoke to him, revealing the wisdom inherent in nature.

Animals have wisdom of a certain kind; their instincts are wise. However, they do not individually possess a soul. Animals share a group soul that as spiritual wisdom influences them from outside. All animals whose blood can be mixed without ill effect have a common soul, that is, a group soul. Wisdom thus acting from outside has become individualized in humans. Every human being has his own individual soul whose influence comes from within. The price human beings pay is loss of certainty. Uncertainty is characteristic of human knowledge and scientific pursuit. Human beings are obliged to grope their way; they must search, select and experiment. However, they have the possibility to evolve, to reach higher stages; the knowledge they are obliged to attain through effort, through trial and error, they can transform so that it becomes wisdom once more. What is already in existence must, as it were, become recast within human beings, must become color-filled, light-filled, sound-filled imagination; then they attain wisdom.

Paracelsus had attained such wisdom; he approached every plant, every chemical substance and instantly recognized its healing properties. An animal immediately knows, through its unconscious instincts, what is beneficial for it. Paracelsus knew through *conscious* wisdom that illness would benefit from a particular substance.

The Therapeutae and Essenes[1] had the same kind of wisdom. It is insight that cannot be attained through experiments; knowledge is transformed into imaginative wisdom. The plant then discerns its own image in the human soul and changes it; in that instant the human being not only senses, but also knows what healing properties the plant possesses. Spiritual science has no objections to natural science; in fact, no one who is serious in his spiritual scientific striving will neglect to acquaint himself with the achievements of ordinary science; he will, however, go further; he will transform such knowledge into creative wisdom. We know that the human being consists of physical body, ether body, astral body and the "I." Ordinary knowledge penetrates only as far as the astral body of which it becomes a part, whereas imaginative knowledge reaches the ether or life body, filling it with the Life Spirit, making human beings powerful healers.

The immense difference between the effect of abstract concepts and that of imaginative knowledge is easiest to see in an incident where the effect was painful in nature: A man was present when his brother had a leg amputated. As the bone was cut it made a strange sound; at that moment the man felt a fierce pain in his leg at the place corresponding to where his brother's operation was taking place. For a long time he could not rid himself of the pain, even when his brother no longer felt any. The sound emitted from the bone had, through the power of imagination, impressed itself deeply into the man's ether body and produced the pain.

A physician in Berne once made an interesting experiment. He took an ordinary horseshoe and connected to it two wires of the type used in electrical machinery. Everyone thought the gadget must be electrified, and those who touched it were certain they felt an electric current; there were even some who were convinced they experienced a violent shock. All these effects were produced simply by what the persons concerned imagined to themselves; no remonstration convinced them otherwise. People became rich by manufacturing pills from ordinary bread. The pills were supposed to cure all kinds of illnesses, but were especially popular for curing sleeplessness. A lady, a patient in a sanatorium, took such a pill regularly every evening and enjoyed sound sleep. One night she decided to take her own life and swallowed as many of these pills as she could lay her hands on. It was discovered, and the doctors were greatly alarmed; she showed all the signs of someone dying. One doctor remained calm, the one who had manufactured the pills.

Human beings have a natural ability to turn the merely known into vivid images. Hypnotism relies on this fact. The hypnotist excludes the astral body and introduces a pictorial content directly into the ether body, but this is an abnormal process. The pictures we ourselves produce are imprinted on the ether body. If they are derived from the spiritual world they have the power to eradicate unhealthy conditions, which means that harmony is brought about with universal spiritual currents. This brings about healing because unhealthy conditions always originate from egoism, and we are now lifted above our ordinary mental life, which is dimmed. This process must occur every so often, for example during sleep; then the astral body, together with the "I," separates from the physical and etheric bodies and unites with the spirit of the earth. From this spiritual region the astral body imprints health-giving pictures into the ether body. This process is unconscious except in highly evolved human beings.

It was Plato who said that eternal ideas are behind everything. The clairvoyant sees the spiritual in every plant whose very form is built up from such spiritual images. These eternal ideas, these spiritual images, human beings are able to absorb and thus become creative. Their health-giving effect acts throughout nature. Strictly speaking, it is only a human being that becomes ill; only people take the spirit into their inner being and must bring it to life once more. Imaginative wisdom will bring a person health. When knowledge is transformed into wisdom, the spirit creates the imagination. Spiritual science is such wisdom, and has the ability more than anything else to be a healing force, especially in the sense of preventing illness. This, admittedly, is not easy to prove. However, through spiritual science, life-giving forces flow into human beings keeping them youthful and strong.

Wisdom makes a person open and receptive because it is a foundation from which love for all things grows. To preach love is useless. (The Therapeutae and Essenes were wise; they were also most compassionate and loving.) When wisdom warms the soul, love streams forth; thus we can understand that there are people who can heal through the laying on of hands. Wisdom pours forces of love through their limbs. Christ was the wisest and therefore also the greatest healer.

Unless love and compassion unite with wisdom, no genuine help can be forthcoming. If someone lying in the street with a broken leg is surrounded by people full of compassion, but without knowledge, they cannot help. The doctor who comes with knowledge of how to deal with a broken leg can help, for his wisdom transforms his compassion into action. Basic to all help provided by human beings is knowledge, insight and ability.

We are always surrounded by wisdom because wise beings created the world. When this wisdom has reached its climax it will have become all-encompassing love. Love will stream towards us from the world of the future. Love is born of wisdom, and the wisest Spiritual Being is the greatest healer. From Christ is born the Holy, that is, the Healing Spirit.

Lecture X

Stages in Man's Development in the Light of Spiritual Science

Berlin, February 28, 1907

The saying above the ancient Greek Temple: "Know Thyself," has resounded to mankind down the ages like a summons to earnest self-introspection. And indeed it expresses one of the greatest truths, but even more than other great truths it is all too easily misunderstood. The real meaning points to something powerful and universal. Originally it neither suggested that a person should contemplate his ordinary everyday self, nor expect to find the sum total of all knowledge within his own being. Rightly understood, the call is for knowledge of the higher self.

But where is a person's higher self to be found? We can by means of a comparison make clear where the higher self exists, and what the saying means: We know for certain that without eyes we would not perceive light; it is, however, equally certain that we would not have eyes had the light flooding all space not first created them. Out of an originally lower organism without sight, knowing only darkness, the light enticed forth the eyes. Hence the truth of Goethe's saying: "The eyes are created by the light for the light." However, the purpose of the eyes is not to perceive themselves. From the point of view of the eye, we must say that they fulfill their task all the better the more they forget themselves and recognize their creator—the light.

The true mission of the eyes is to forget their inner being and recognize what created them, that is what to the eyes is the higher self—the light. The situation is the same in regard to a person's ordinary self; that too is nothing but an organ, a tool; and self-knowledge becomes ever greater the more *this* self can forget itself and become aware of the spirit-light, existing in the eternal world, that created our spiritual eyes and continually does so. Therefore, self-knowledge rightly understood means self-development. This we must keep in mind and see as background to today's lecture, which concerns the subject of self-knowledge in the highest sense of the word.

Taking all aspects of an individual's nature into consideration, let us look at the way he evolves during his life between birth and death. In so doing, we must not forget that when a person starts his life on earth he is not a newly created entity; he brings certain qualities with him. Repeated earth lives are behind him, during which the fundamental character of his individuality has already been established. We must consider a person's existence after death if we are to recognize what he brings with him through birth. That existence will reveal what he has retained throughout the time between death and new birth, and so brings with him into a new life.

Let us remind ourselves that at death the human being leaves behind only the physical corpse. The main difference between death and sleep is that the human being asleep possesses a physical and an etheric body;

only the astral body and what we call "I" are lifted out. Just as an architect is needed to create a building, as the bricks do not come together of themselves, so do the physical forces need the ether body as an inner architect. The ether body holds together the physical matter and forces from birth to death. At every moment it prevents the chemical combinations from falling apart. But at death it leaves the physical body, which consequently is left behind as the decaying corpse. Thus, in sleep it is only the "I" and astral body, the bearer of pleasure and pain, cravings and sentiments, that leaves, whereas in death the ether body also leaves and remains with the astral body and the "I" for a short time. This is an important moment in a person's existence. During that short time there passes before the human soul with lightning speed a mighty memory tableau of his whole past life. This tableau is like a painting, and just as we do not feel the stab of the dagger depicted in a painting, so do we not experience either pleasure or pain in what the tableau portrays. We stand before our past life as objective observer.

Then comes the time when the ether body withdraws and disperses into the general world ether. However, something of the ether body remains, which is like an extract or a summary of the past life. The tableau becomes indistinct and dissolves, but the extract remains united with a person throughout his further journey. In fact, an essence or extract also remains of the physical body, which is of course not something that can be seen with physical sight; it is like a center of energy that remains with the ether body; it is what gives the physical body its human form.

After the ether body has dissolved, the astral body still remains. An individual now passes through a condition during which he gradually adjusts to being without a physical environment. We must realize that everything a person has experienced as lower enjoyment clings to the astral body. The physical body has no cravings; it experiences no pleasure, but is the instrument that enables the astral body to obtain enjoyment. Take the case of a gourmet. It is not the physical body that enjoys the food, but the astral body that uses the physical body as a tool to enjoy it. The craving remains after the physical body is laid aside, but now the tool for obtaining satisfaction is lacking. This indicates the nature of the astral body's existence after death, comparable to someone suffering thirst in a region for the length and breadth of which there is no water. Instincts, cravings and passions are now felt by the astral body as burning thirst, not because the objects of its desires are not there, but because the organs are lacking through which satisfaction can be obtained. That is why religion speaks of the ordeal by fire that human beings undergo after death.

The human being remains in kamaloca for as long as the astral body retains a longing for the physical body. Gradually it frees itself of its dependence on what surrounded it when clothed in a physical body. Someone who has purified his passions already during life, so that instead of coarser enjoyments he takes pleasure in what is beautiful, artistic and spiritual, will shorten his time kamaloca. On the other hand, those who only find pleasure in things for which a physical tool is needed will remain a long time in the region of burning thirst. Eventually what is not purified falls away like a kind of astral corpse, comparable to what is left behind of the physical and etheric bodies. The more of the astral body a person has purified, the more he is able to retain and add to the extracts from the physical and etheric bodies.

With these three extracts, a person passes into the

essentially spiritual world where everything the "I" has experienced and has acquired during earthly life is perfected. Some people enter life possessing great talents, discernible already in childhood, and only waiting to be brought out. A person can bring such talents because his earthly experiences were transformed into abilities during his sojourn in Spirit Land.

In the course of each life on earth, a person adds something new to the extracts of his three bodies. If a person is born with special talents, it shows that he has made good use of his former lives. He has as it were added many pages to the record of his experiences and achievements. When he enters a new life he receives a physical body from physical ancestors. The core of his being, bringing the fruits of former experiences, is drawn to a family that can provide the physical characteristics he needs for making use of the already acquired capabilities. The characteristics a person inherits do not determine his actions or his abilities; all they provide is the tool with which to express them. However, the tool is essential. A master pianist needs an instrument, and so does the incarnating individuality. If a person is to express himself properly in the physical world, the new body that clothes him must be the right tool. This tends to give rise to the mistaken view that everything is inherited. Heredity certainly plays a part, but only insofar as the incarnating individuality feels drawn to parents that can provide him with the most suitable tool.

Everything as yet not purified that was left behind at different stages gathers again about the person. He must receive it back in order to continue the purification of the being.

We have already discussed various aspects of what takes place during the first half of a person's life. In order to see how his fate and fortune in later life depends upon the way his physical, etheric and astral bodies develop during the first half, we must repeat some aspects connected with school life and education that reach further completion in the second half. This is an important issue, and it is essential to recognize certain significant laws. These are laws that apply in general, though they may become modified in various ways. In order to adjust properly to life and recognize one's destination ever more clearly, the working of these laws must be understood.

Let us begin with birth. We know that at physical birth only the physical body is fully born. The organs could develop before birth because the embryo is completely protected by the surrounding maternal sheath. Only when this is pushed aside is this body exposed to the physical elements. The ether body is not born yet, even less the astral body; they are still surrounded by an etheric and an astral sheath. These sheaths, visible only to spiritual sight, are not part of a person's own nature, but they envelop and protect him. At the change of teeth in the seventh year when the ether body is born, the etheric sheath is pushed aside as was the maternal body at physical birth. And only at puberty is the astral body born and fully exposed to the influences of the external world.

It must be realized that in the first seven years of life only what is described as the essence or extract of the former physical body is freed; this is what gives the physical its form, guiding its structural development. The organs grow larger, but their shape and function are inherent in them. It is of the greatest importance that everything in the environment of the growing child enables the physical structure to unfold in the best possible way. The essential aspect of this period can be summed up in two significant words: *imitation* and *example*. At this age the child imitates everything that goes on or exists around him. It is this activity of imitation that coaxes the inner organs to develop their inherent form. The brain of a seven-year old may still be incomplete, but the foundation for the child's further development is laid, and any lack cannot be made up later. The appearance of the second teeth marks the end of the activity of the physical principle, which is the principle of structure and form. The teeth are the outwardly visible sign that the bones and joints and also the softer organs have consolidated. The influence of light is what entices the power of sight to the surface in the eyes.

As already mentioned, it is best not to give children perfect dolls and similar toys. A healthy child will only get pleasure from it for a short while. A knot in a table napkin with indications of eyes and ears will provide far more pleasure; this is because the child's fantasy becomes active in providing what the doll lacks. This encourages the development of the inner organs; they become strong, as a muscle becomes strong when activated. The environment should provide happiness, pleasure and enjoyment because it calls up in the child inner feelings and activity that flow like strong up-building forces through its organs. A bad environment at this time in the child's life does more to harm the organs than anything else. The notion, based on false asceticism, that the child benefits from being accustomed to an austere, lackluster existence is utterly wrong. As regards nourishment, if the child is given the right food it will develop a liking for what is beneficial, whereas wrong food will cause sickness.

Through spiritual science we can gain insight into what would be done at every age. Thus, we must be clear that as the physical principle is at work in the first seven years, and should be left undisturbed, our primary concern must be to do what is right and healthy for the child's bodily nature. Regarding nutrition it must be realized that there exists a spiritual bond between mother and child, especially during the early years; the mother who breast-feeds her child pays heed to this relationship. The milk contains more than its physical, chemical components; spiritually it is related to the child. It is evident from spiritual research that the milk issues from the mother's ether body. Because the child's own ether body is not born yet, it can at first only tolerate what has been prepared by another ether body. Statistical evidence shows that of those who die in infancy, 16 to 20 percent have been breast-fed by their own mother, while 26 to 30 percent have not. This is an indication of the close affinity between the ether bodies. The affinity expresses itself physically in family likeness. Traits and characteristics pointing to the line of descent develop and become established during the first years.

What is of paramount importance from the seventh to the fourteenth year can also be summed up in two significant words: *emulation* and *authority*. This is the time when it is essential that the evolving human being can look up to someone who for him or her incorporates all that is good, beautiful and wise. To the child this person must be the embodiment of everything contained in maxims and precepts. Preaching moral axioms has far less effect than presenting to the child ideal examples to emulate—examples showing the path to Olympus. To be able at this age to look up to someone with feelings of deepest reverence and respect is of great significance for the rest of a person's life. What matters here is of course the emulation. This is why the teaching of history should be so conducted that figures illustrating wisdom and strength of character are brought before the child. From descriptions of the characteristics of a folk or a race, one proceeds to descriptions of individuals where ancestry no longer plays a part. Emulation of relatives widens to become emulation of strangers. The child's horizon expands through awareness of other people; the ether body also widens beyond its own race and clan.

Whereas before the change of teeth, features that show family likeness become defined, now when the child's life widens beyond the family circle, his gestures, that is, what is distinctly individual, become characteristic. At this time the etheric sheath dissolves. Influence can now be brought to bear on the ether body. This influence should come from people who, because of what they themselves are, can bring out the attributes stored in the child's ether body. Furthermore, now that the ether body, after the seventh year, is no longer restricted, those basic traits, the fruits brought over from former incarnations, begin to develop. Consequently, a true principle of education demands that the educator should now, as it were, stand back and consider just what it is the child has brought over; for thanks to the freed ether body the organs should now become stronger and increase in size.

Up to the seventh year physical forces elaborated and plastically formed the organs, but now our task is to instill into these organs, as they grow larger, all the attributes related to the ether body, such as conscience, energy and morality. Everything we bring the child must be pictorial and imbued with a pure spiritual delight in the world, for these are qualities that must be so deeply imprinted that they become part of the ether body. If the human being is to develop a strong character, his ether body must be able to evolve unimpeded. The educator must at this time say to himself: What I am dealing with is not something to be molded arbitrarily; I may do irrevocable harm unless I pay heed to what the child has brought over from the ether body of his former life. This is also the reason why it is important that physical exercises produce a feeling in the child of growing strength and increase of stature. The child should experience a sensation of growing, not just physically, but morally. These feelings work plastically on the ether body, as the physical principle did earlier on the physical body.

The astral attributes which an individual brings with him develop while the astral body is still surrounded by its astral sheath, as did the physical organs while still surrounded by the maternal body before birth. Only when puberty is reached does the astral body become free, that is, become open to external influence. Only now should appeal be made to the power of judgment and abstract thought. Before puberty the child should not be obliged to form personal opinions and judgments. The ability to do so is not present until the astral body is born. Before puberty the child should be able to look up to those with authority and obtain from them the important beliefs and opinions; to be obliged to formulate personal opinion at this time only leads to astral distortions. Not only is it absurd for anyone so young to have opinions about this or that belief or confession, but it is also detrimental to healthy development. It is a sign that something important has been neglected in his education. It shows the child has not had the opportunity to develop that great inner strength that matures under the influence of the right kind of authority. At this time, from the fourteenth year onwards, when the astral body is born, slowly and gradually the power of judgment begins to ripen and leads to convictions. Artistic accomplishment, religious and moral feelings now set their stamp on the countenance. A child now faces the world as a distinct individual. This gradual process lasts up to the twenty-first or twenty-third year.

It is an important moment when at the time of puberty awareness of other people as individuals awakens. Just as: "All that is transient but as symbol is sent," so too is the becoming aware of the other sex symbolic. Only now does the human being attain a personal relationship to the world; thus, love of the individual awakens. Up to then the relationships are more universally human, whereas now personal judgment plays a part. The astral extract a person brought over into life is now freed and able to develop. It comes to expression as high ideals, beautiful hopes and expectations of life, all of which are forces that are essential to human beings. A person's development will take the right course if, rather than having something external imposed upon him, his inherent inclinations and talents are brought out during his school days. Ideals are not simply there; they originate in forces that are astir within youth which at this time strive for expression. Nothing is worse for later life than an absence of feelings of great hopes and expectations; right up into the twenties, they constitute real forces. The more we are able to bring out a person's inner inclinations and talents brought over from former lives, the more we benefit his development. Not until the twenty-third year does this come to an end; then a person is ready to begin his "years of apprenticeship" (*Wanderjahre*). Only now is the "I" born; only now does a person face the world as an independent personality.

Now is the "I," as a result of collaboration with his four members, in direct contact with the world. The fruits of former life experiences no longer have to be inwardly developed; an individual is ripe to face the reality of the world. If a person is obliged to do so earlier, his best talents and abilities are spoiled; the essence brought over as forces is deadened. It is a sin against youth if the person is exposed to the prosaic aspects of life at an earlier age. Now a person matures; the time has come when that individual is truly able to learn from life. He approaches his "years of mastery" (*Meisterjahren*) between his twenty-eighth and thirty-fifth years. However, these time limits must not be taken too rigidly.

About the thirty-fifth year a human being reaches the middle of life. Those with spiritual insight have always regarded this age as extremely important. They have recognized that, while up to the twenty-first year a person evolves, the talents and abilities contained as predispositions in his three bodies—and up to the twenty-eighth year what the world offers him—now at the age of thirty-five he begins to work on his three bodies. First of all a person strengthens the astral body. Up till now the world has taught him, but now his judgment begins to carry weight with his fellowmen. It would be well if his opinions have not been so far too definite, too conclusive; they should not become consolidated until about the age of thirty-five. From now on the astral body becomes ever denser; if up till now the person has been a learner, he or she can now become an adviser. A person's judgments have significance and are taken into account when problems are in the balance. The apprentice has become counselor.

After the thirty-fifth year and beyond, the astral body influences the "I," the blood and the nervous system; it acts on growth and has a stabilizing, consolidating effect that results in a certain firmness. What a human being absorbs in his life of thoughts and feelings of a spiritual nature comes to expression as cultural interest and courage. One could therefore also call this "a period when the systems of blood and nerves are elaborated." It all comes to an end physically when the ether body begins to withdraw its activity from the external aspect of the physical body, at about the thirty-fifth year. It is also the reason why a human then ceases to grow; a person solidifies, fat begins to be deposited; the strength of the muscles diminishes. It all stems from the fact that the ether body is withdrawing. However, it also means that forces are released as they no longer have to work on the physical body. They can now unite with what has inwardly been elaborated: a person becomes wise. It was well-known in ancient times that in public life a person's counsel could not be of value until the ether body began to withdraw from the physical body. Only then was a person ready to enter public life; only then could his or her talents be of benefit to the people and the state.

Human beings withdraw more and more into their inner being after the thirty-fifth year. No longer does a person have the longings and expectations of youth; he is instead capable of judgment, which one feels carries weight. At the same time certain abilities connected with the ether body, such as memory, begin to wane. About the fiftieth year the physical principle also begins to withdraw. More and more calcium is deposited while the tissue becomes slack. The withdrawing physical principle gradually unites with the etheric principle; what has gone into the bones, muscles, blood and nerves begins to develop a life of its own. The human being becomes more and more spiritual. All this is certainly greatly enhanced and furthered if the early education was right, particularly as far as the astral body is concerned. Unless the astral body has experienced youthful joy and expectation, it will not now contain what it should be able to imprint on the denser ether body. If that is lacking, then the strong inner life described cannot unfold. We find instead what is called the "childishness of old age." People who in their youth failed to be imbued with fresh vigorous forces will begin in old age to dry up. It is especially important to take note of this fact from the point of view of spiritual science.

With the thirty-fifth year, the most favorable time arrives for attaining spiritual insight and developing spiritual faculties. A person's karma is particularly auspicious when this does not happen too late in life. The forces that otherwise flow into the bodily nature are becoming free and are at our disposal. As long as a person is obliged to direct his forces outwards, he cannot direct them inwards; that is why the age of about thirty-five is the most favorable time for developing spiritual insight. Development in the first half of life proceeds according to specific time sequences; as indicated by spiritual science, they also exist in the second half, but are not so sharply defined.

Human beings begin to work towards the future in the second half of life. What they inwardly develop at an older age becomes in the future organ and body-building forces; later they participate in cosmic forces. What will thus exist in the future is already indicated in the first half of life. Young people in particular may find this division oppressive; not, however, if spiritual science has been absorbed and understood. When human life is surveyed from a higher viewpoint, it is precisely through such details that one gains practical insight into life's requirements. One must have patience and be able to wait until the organs that are necessary in a particular sphere have developed.

Lecture XI

Who are the Rosicrucians?

Berlin, March 14, 1907

Today's subject, the Rosicrucians, is one which few people are able to connect even remotely adequate ideas. And indeed, it is not easy to arrive at anything conclusive about what the name implies. For most people it remains extremely vague. If books are consulted, one is informed that the Rosicrucians are thought to be some kind of sect that flourished in the early centuries of German culture. Some say that it is impossible to verify whether anything serious or rational ever existed behind the fraud and charlatanry associated with the name. On the other hand, some learned books do proffer a variety of information.

If what is written about Rosicrucianism is true, one could only come to the conclusion that it has consisted of nothing but idle boasting, pure fraud or worse. Even those who have attempted to justify it, do so with an air of patronage, though they may have found that Rosicrucianism is able to throw light on certain subjects. But what they have to say about it, for example, that it is involved with alchemy, with producing the philosopher's stone, the stone of the wise, and other alchemical feats, does not inspire much confidence.

However, these feats were for the genuine Rosicrucian nothing but symbols for the inner moral purification of the human soul. The transformations represented symbolically how inner human virtues should be developed. When the Rosicrucians spoke of transforming base metals into gold, they meant that it was possible to transform base vices into the gold of human virtue.

Those who uphold that the great work of the Rosicrucians is to be understood as being symbolic are met with the objection that in that case Rosicrucianism is simply trivial. It is difficult to see the need of all these alchemical inventions, such as the transformation of metals, simply to demonstrate the obvious fact that a human being should be moral and change his vices into virtues.

However, Rosicrucianism contains things of far greater import. Rather than further historical description, I shall give a factual account of Rosicrucianism. The historical aspect need concern us only insofar as we learn from it that Rosicrucianism has existed in the Occident since the fourteenth century, and that it goes back to a legendary figure, Christian Rosenkreuz,[1] about whom much is rumored, but history has little to say.

One incident that appears as a basic feature of various accounts can be summed up by saying that Christian Rosenkreuz—that is not his real name, but the one by which he is known—made journeys at the end of the fifteenth and the beginning of the sixteenth centuries. On journeys through the East he became acquainted with the book M———, a book from which, so we are mysteriously told, Paracelsus, the great medieval physician and mystic, gained his knowledge. This account is true, but what the book M——— actually is, and what study of it signifies, is known only to initiates.

External information about Rosicrucianism stems from two writings that appeared at the beginning of the seventeenth century, the so-called *Fama Fraternitatis* in 1614, and a year later the *Confessio*, two books much disputed among scholars. The disputes were by no means confined to the usual controversy about books, that is, whether Valentin Andreae,[2] who in his later years was an ordinary normal clergyman, was really the author. In this case it was also disputed whether the author meant the books to be taken seriously or whether they were meant as satire, mocking a certain secret brotherhood known as the Rosicrucians. These two publications were followed by many others proffering all kinds of information about Rosicrucianism.

Someone without knowledge of the true background of Rosicrucianism, who picks up the writings of Valentin Andreae, or indeed any other Rosicrucian document, will find nothing exceptional in them. In fact, right up to our own time, it has been impossible to gain even elementary knowledge of this spiritual stream that still exists, and has done so since the fourteenth century. Everything published, written or printed is nothing but fragments, lost through betrayal into public hands. Not only are these fragments inaccurate; they have undergone all kinds of distortions through charlatanry, fraud, incomprehension and sheer stupidity. As long as it has existed, genuine Rosicrucianism has been passed on by word of mouth to members sworn to secrecy. That is also why nothing of great importance has found its way into public literature.

We shall speak today about certain elementary aspects of Rosicrucianism that can now be spoken of in public, for reasons which at the moment would take us too far to explain. Only when they are known can one make any sense of what is found in the often grotesque, often merely comic, but also often fraudulent, and seldom accurate information.

Rosicrucianism is one of the methods whereby what is called "initiation" can be attained. What initiation is has often been a subject of discussion in our circles. To be initiated means that faculties slumbering in every human soul are awakened. These faculties enable a person to look into the spiritual world that exists behind our physical world. The physical world is an expression of the spiritual world of which it is a product. An initiate is someone who has applied the method of initiation, a method as exact and as scientifically worked out as those applied in chemistry, physics or any other science. The difference is that the method of initiation is not applied to begin with to anything external, but only to the human being; he is the instrument, the tool through which knowledge of the spiritual world is attained. An individual who genuinely strives to attain knowledge of the spirit recognizes the deep truth contained in Goethe's words:

> Mysterious by Day's broad light,
> Nature retains her veil, despite our clamors,
> and what she won't reveal to human mind or sight
> Cannot be wrenched from her with levers, screws
> or hammers.*

Deep indeed are the secrets nature holds, but not as impenetrably deep as those maintain who are too comfortable to make the effort. The human spirit is certainly capable of penetrating nature's secrets: not, however, through the soul's ordinary faculties, but

---

* *Faust*, Part I, Night. trans. Bayard Taylor.

146

through higher ones, attained when its hidden forces have been developed through certain strictly circumscribed methods. A person who gradually prepares will eventually reach a point where knowledge attainable only through initiation is revealed to him; to speak in Goethe's sense: The great secret is revealed of what "ultimately holds the world together"—a revelation that is truly a fruit of initiation.

It has often been explained that the early stages of initiation can be embarked upon by anyone without any danger whatever. A prerequisite for the higher stages is the very highest conscientiousness and devotion to Truth in spiritual research. When an individual approaches the portals through which he looks into quite different worlds, he realizes the truth of what is often emphasized: that it is dangerous to impart the holy secrets of existence to great masses of people. However, to the extent that modern humanity is able, through inner preparation, gradually to find their way to the highest secrets of nature and the spiritual world, to that extent can they also be revealed.

The spiritual scientific movement is a path that guides human beings to the higher secrets. A number of such paths exist. That is not to say that the ultimate truth attainable takes different forms. The highest truth is *one*. No matter where or when human beings ever lived or live, once they reach the highest Truth, it is the same for all. It is comparable to the view from the mountaintop, which is the same for all who reach it, no matter what different paths they choose to get there. When one stands at a certain spot on the mountainside, when a path is available, one does not walk round the mountain for another path. The same applies to the path of higher knowledge, which must be in accordance with a person's nature. What comes into consideration here is too often overlooked, that is, the immense differences in human nature. The people of ancient India were inwardly organized differently from modern people. This difference in the higher members is apparent to spiritual research, though not to the external science of physiology or anatomy. It is thanks to this fact that we have preserved up to our own time a wonderful spiritual knowledge, and also the method whereby initiation was achieved—the path of yoga. This path leads those who are constituted like the people of ancient India to the summit of knowledge. For today's European it is as senseless to seek that path as it would be to first walk to the opposite side of the mountain and use the path there rather than the path available where one stands. The nature of today's European is completely different from that of the Oriental. A few centuries before the Christian era began, human nature was different from what it was to become a few centuries later. And today it is different again.

As we have seen, initiation is based upon awakening in human beings certain forces. Bearing this in mind, we must acknowledge that a person's nature must be taken into account when methods are developed whereby he becomes the instrument able to perceive and to investigate the spiritual world.

The wonderful method developed by the Rishis, the great spiritual teachers in ancient India, is still valid for those belonging to the Indian race. At the beginning of the Christian era the right method was the so-called Christian-Gnostic path. The human being who stands fully within today's civilization needs a different method. That is why in the course of centuries and millennia the great masters of wisdom who guide mankind's evolution change the methods that lead to the summit of wisdom.

The Rosicrucian method of initiation is especially for modern people; it meets the needs of modern conditions. Not only is it a Christian path, but it enables the striving human being to recognize that spiritual research and its achievements are in complete harmony with modern culture, and with modern humanity's whole outlook. It will for long centuries to come be the right method of initiation into spiritual life. When it was first inaugurated, certain rules were laid down for its adherents—rules that are basically still valid, and because they are strictly observed, Rosicrucians are not recognized by outsiders. Never to let it be known that one is a Rosicrucian is the first rule that only recently has been slightly modified. While the wisdom is fostered in narrow circles, its fruits should be available to all humanity. That is why until recently no Rosicrucian divulged what enabled him to investigate nature's secrets. Nothing of the knowledge was revealed; no hint was given theoretically or otherwise, but work was done that furthered civilization and implanted wisdom in ways hardly noticeable to others.

That is the first basic rule; to elaborate it further would lead too far. Suffice it to say that today this rule has been partly relaxed, but the higher Rosicrucian knowledge is not revealed. The second rule concerns conduct, and may be expressed as follows: Be truly part of the civilization and people to which you belong; be a member of the class in which you find yourself. Wear the clothes that are worn generally, nothing different or conspicuous. Thus, you will find that neither ambition nor selfishness motivates the Rosicrucian; he rather strives wherever possible to improve aspects of the prevailing culture, while never losing sight of the much loftier aims that link him with the central Rosicrucian wisdom.

The other basic rules need not concern us at the moment. We want to look at the actual Rosicrucian training as it still exists and has existed for centuries. What it is possible to say about it deals only with the elementary stages of the whole system of Rosicrucian schooling. Something ought to be said about this training that applies to spiritual scientific training, namely, that it should not be embarked upon without knowledgeable guidance. What is to be said about this subject you will find in my book *Knowledge of Higher Worlds and its Attainment*.

The preliminary Rosicrucian training consists of seven stages that need not be absolved in the sequence here enumerated. The teacher will lay more emphasis on one point or another, according to the pupil's individuality and special needs. Thus, it is a path of learning and inner development, adapted to the particular pupil. These are the seven steps:

1. Study, in the Rosicrucian sense of the word
2. Acquisition of imaginative knowledge
3. Acquisition of the occult script
4. Bringing rhythm into life, this is also described as preparing the philosopher's stone. This has nothing in common with the nonsense written about it.
5. Knowledge of the microcosm, that is, of man's essential nature
6. Becoming one with the macrocosm or great world
7. Attaining godliness (*Gottseligkeit*).

The sequence in which the student passes through these preliminary stages of Rosicrucian training depends on the students personality, but they must be absolved. What I have said about it so far, and also what I am going to say, must be looked upon as describing the ideal. Do not think that these things can be attained from one day to the next. However, one can at least learn the description of what today may seem a far distant goal. A start can always be made provided it is realized that patience, energy and perseverance are required.

The first stage or *study*, suggests to many something dry and pedantic. But in this case what is meant has nothing to do with erudition in the usual sense. One need not be a scholar to be an initiate. Spiritual knowledge and scholarship have no close connection. What is here meant by study is something rather different, but absolutely essential; and no genuine teacher of Rosicrucianism will guide the pupil to the higher stages if the student has no aptitude for what this first stage demands. It requires the student to develop a thinking that is thoroughly sensible and logical. This is necessary if the pupil is not to lose the ground under his feet at the higher stages. From the start it must be made clear that, unless all inclination towards fantasy and illusion is overcome, it is all too easy to fall into error when striving to enter spiritual realms. A person who is inclined to see things in a fanciful or unreal light is of no use to the spiritual world.

That is one reason; another is that though a person is born from the astral world, that is from the spiritual world next to the physical, as much as he is born from the physical world, what he experiences there is completely different from anything seen with physical sight or heard with physical ears. One thing, however, is the same in all three worlds—in the physical, the astral or spiritual, and the devachanic world—and that is logical thinking. It is precisely because it is the same in all three worlds that it can be learned already in the physical world, and thus provide a firm support when we enter the other worlds. If one's thoughts are like will-o-the-wisps so that no distinction is made between what is merely depicted and reality, then one is not qualified to rise into higher worlds. This happens for example in modern physics when the atom, which no one has even seen, is spoken of as if it were a material reality.

However, what we are discussing now is not what is generally meant by thinking. Ordinary thinking consists of combining physical facts. Here we are concerned with thinking that has become sense-free. Today there are learned people, including philosophers, who deny the existence of such thinking. Modern philosophers of great renown tell us that human beings cannot think in pure thoughts, only in thoughts that reflect something physical. Such a statement simply shows that the person concerned is not capable of thinking in pure thoughts. However, it is the height of arrogance to maintain that something is impossible just because one cannot accomplish it oneself. Human beings must be able to formulate thoughts that are not dependent on what is seen or heard physically. A person must be able to find himself in a world of pure thought when his attention is completely withdrawn from external reality. In spiritual science, and also in Rosicrucianism, this is known as self-created thinking. Someone who resolves to train his thinking in this direction may turn to books on spiritual science. There he will not find a thinking that combines physical facts, but thoughts derived from higher worlds, which present a self-sustaining continuous thinking. And as anyone can follow it, the reader is able to rise above the ordinary trivial way of thinking.

In order to make accessible the elementary stages of Rosicrucianism, it was necessary to make available in print and through lectures, material that had for centuries been guarded in closed circles. However, what has been released in recent decades is only the rudiments of an immeasurable, far-reaching world knowledge. In the course of time more and more will flow into mankind. Study of this material schools the pupil's thinking. For those who seek a still stricter schooling, my books *Truth and Knowledge* and *The Philosophy of Freedom* are particularly suitable. Those two books are not written like other books; no sentence can be placed anywhere but where it stands. Each of the books represents, not a collection of thoughts, but a thought-organism. Thought is not added to thought, each grows organically from the preceding one, like growth occurs in an organism. The thoughts must necessarily develop in like manner in the reader. In this way a person makes his own thinking with the characteristic that is self-generating. Without this kind of thinking the higher stages of Rosicrucianism cannot be attained. However, a study of the basic spiritual scientific literature will also school thinking; the more thorough schooling is not absolutely necessary in order to absolve the first stage of Rosicrucian training.

The second stage is the *acquisition of imaginative thinking.* This should only be attempted when the stage of study has been absolved, so that one possesses an inner foundation of knowledge and has made one's own thoughts that follow one another out of inner necessity. Without such a foundation it is all too easy to lose the ground under one's feet. But what is meant by imaginative thinking?

Goethe, who in his poem, *The Mysteries*, showed his profound knowledge of Rosicrucianism, gave a hint at what imaginative thinking was, in the words uttered by the Chorus Mysticus, in the second part of *Faust:* "All things transitory but as symbols are sent." The knowledge that everything transitory was mere symbol was systematically cultivated wherever a Rosicrucian training was pursued. A Rosicrucian had to acquire an insight that recognizes in everything, something spiritual and eternal. In addition to ordinary knowledge of what he encountered on his journeys through life, a Rosicrucian had to acquire imaginative knowledge as well.

When someone meets you with a smiling face, you do not stop short at the characteristic contortion of his features, you see beyond the physiognomic expression and recognize that the smile reveals the person's inner life. Likewise you recognize tears to be an expression of inner pain and sorrow. In other words, the outer expresses the inner; through the physiognomy you perceive the depths of soul. A Rosicrucian has to learn this in regard to the whole of nature. As the human face, or the gesture of a hand, is the expression of a person's soul life, so, for the Rosicrucian, everything that takes place in nature is an expression of soul and spirit. Every stone, plant and animal, every current of air, the stars, all express soul and spirit just as do shining eyes, a wrinkled brow or tears. If you do not stop short at today's materialistic interpretation that regards what the Earth-Spirit says in Goethe's *Faust* as poetic fantasy, but recognize that it depicts reality, then you know what is meant by imaginative knowledge.

> In the tides of life, in action's storm,
> A fluctuant wave,
> A shuttle free,
> Birth and the Grave,
> An eternal sea.
> A weaving, flowing
> Life, all-glowing,

> Thus at time's humming loom 'tis my hand
> prepares
> The garment of Life which the Deity wears!

If for you these words of the Earth-Spirit depict spiritual reality, then you will know that you possess a deeper logic, and can calmly accept being called a fool by materialists who only think they understand. As the human physiognomy expresses the life of the human soul, so does the physiognomy of the earth express the life of the Earth-Spirit. When you begin to read in nature, when nature reveals its mysteries, and different plants convey to you the Earth-Spirit's cheerfulness or sorrow, then you begin to understand imaginative knowledge. Then you will also recognize that it is this that is presented as the purest and most beautiful expression of the striving for imaginative knowledge in Rosicrucianism, and also in what preceded Rosicrucianism, the ideal of the Holy Grail.

Let us look for a moment at the true nature of the Holy Grail. This ideal is always found in every Rosicrucian school. The form it takes I shall describe as a conversation which, however, never took place in reality because what I shall summarize could only be attained in the course of long training and development. However, what I shall say does convey what is looked up to as the Quest of the Holy Grail:

Look how the plant grows out of the earth. Its stem strives upward; its roots are sunk into the ground, pointing towards the centre of the earth. The opening blossom contains its reproductive organs, which bear the seeds through which the plant continues beyond itself. Charles Robert Darwin,[3] the famous natural scientist, is not the first to point out that, if a person is compared to the plant, it is the root, not the blossom, that corresponds to his head. This was said already by esoteric Rosicrucianism. The calyx, which chastely strives towards the sun, corresponds to the reproductive organs that in human beings are situated downwards. Human beings are inverted plants. A person turns downwards and covers up in shame the organs that the plant chastely turns upward to the light.

To recognize that the human being is the plant inverted is basic to Rosicrucianism, as indeed to all esoteric knowledge. Human beings turn their reproductive organs towards the centre of the earth; in the plant they turn towards the sun. The plant root points towards the centre of the earth; human beings lift their heads unfettered towards sunlit spaces. The animal occupies a position between the two. The three directions indicated by plant, animal and human are known as the cross. The animal represents the beam across, the plant the downward, the human being the upward pointing section of the vertical beam. Plato, the great philosopher of antiquity, stated that the World-Soul is crucified on the World-Body. He meant that human beings represent the highest development of the World-Soul, which passes through the three kingdoms of plant, animal and human. The World-Soul is crucified on the cross of plants, animal and human kingdoms. These words of Plato are spoken completely in the sense of spiritual science and present a wonderful and deeply significant picture.

The pupil in the Rosicrucian school had repeatedly to bring the picture before his mind of the plant with its head downward and the reproductive organs stretching towards the beam of the sun. The sunbeam was called the "holy lance of love" that must penetrate the plant to enable the seeds to mature and grow. The pupil was told: Contemplate man in relation to the plant; compare the substance of which man is composed with that of the plant. Man, the plant turned upside down, has permeated his substance, his flesh, with physical cravings, passion and sensuality. The plant stretches in purity and chastity the reproductive organs towards the fertilizing sacred lance of love. This stage will be reached by an individual when he has completely purified all cravings. In the future, when earth evolution has reached its height, a person will attain this ideal. When no impure desires permeate the lower organs, a person will become as chaste and pure as the plant is now. That individual will stretch a lance of spiritual love, the completely spiritualized productive force, towards a calyx that opens as does that of the plant to the holy lance of love of the sunbeam.

Thus, the human being's development takes him through the kingdoms of nature. He purifies his being until he develops organs of which there are as yet only indications. The beginning of a future productive power can be seen when human beings create something that is sacred and noble—a force they will fully possess once their lower nature is purified. A new organ will then have developed; the calyx will arise on a higher level and open to the lance of Amfortas, as the plant calyx opens to the sun's spiritual lance of love.

Thus, what the Rosicrucian pupil depicted to himself represents on a lower level the great future ideal of mankind, attainable when the lower nature has been purified and chastely offers itself to the spiritualized sun of the future. Then human nature, which in one sense is higher, in another lower than that of the plant, will have developed within itself the innocence and purity of the plant calyx.

The Rosicrucian pupil grasped all of this in its spiritual meaning. He understood it as the mystery of the Holy

Grail[4]—mankind's highest ideal. He saw the whole of nature permeating and glowing with spiritual meaning. When everything is thus seen as symbol of the spirit, one is on the way to attain imaginative knowledge; color and sound separate from objects and become independent. Space becomes a world of color and sound in which spiritual beings announce their presence. The pupil rises from imaginative knowledge to direct knowledge of the spiritual realm. That is the path of the Rosicrucian pupil at the second stage of training.

The third stage is *knowledge of the occult script*. This is no ordinary writing, but one that is connected with nature's secrets. Let me at once make clear how to depict it. A widely used sign is the so-called vortex, which can be thought of as two intertwined figure 6's. This sign is used for indicating and also characterizing a certain type of event that can occur both physically and spiritually. For example, a developing plant will finally produce seeds from which new plants similar to the old one can develop. To think that anything material passes from the old plant to the new is materialistic prejudice without foundation and will eventually be refuted. What passes over to the new plant is formative forces. As far as matter is concerned, the old plant dies completely; materially its offspring is a completely new creation. This dying and new coming-into-being of the plant is indicated by drawing two intertwining spirals, that is, a vortex, but drawing it so that the two spirals do not touch.

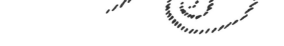

Many events take place, both physical and spiritual,

that correspond to such a vortex. For example, we know from spiritual research that the transition from the ancient Atlantean culture to the first post-Atlantean culture was such a vortex. Natural science only knows the most elementary aspects of this event. Spiritual science tells us that the space between Europe and America, which is now the Atlantic Ocean, was filled with a continent on which an ancient civilization developed, a continent that was submerged by the Flood. This proves that what Plato referred to as the disappearance of the Island of Poseidon is based on facts; the island was part of the ancient Atlantean continent. The spiritual aspect of that ancient culture vanished, and a new culture arose. The vortex is a sign for this event; the inward-turning spiral signifies the old civilization and the outward-turning the new.

As the transition took place from the old culture to the new, the sun rose in spring in the constellation of Cancer—as you know the sun moves forward in the course of the year. Later it rose in early spring in the constellation of Gemini, then in that of Taurus and later still in that of Aries. People have always felt that what reached them from the vault of heaven in the beams of the early spring sun was especially beneficial. This is why people venerated the ram when the spring sun rose in the constellation of Aries; it is also the reason for legends such as "The Golden Fleece" and others. Earlier than that the sun rose in spring in the constellation of Taurus, and we find in ancient Egypt the cult of the bull Apis. But the transition from Atlantis to post-Atlantis took place under the constellation of Cancer, whose sign is the intertwining spirals—a sign you find depicted in calendars.

There exist hundreds and thousands of such signs that the pupil gradually learns. The signs are not arbitrary; they enable those who understand them to immerse themselves in things and directly experience their essence. While study schools the faculty of reason, and imaginative knowledge the life of feelings, knowledge of the occult script takes hold of the will. It is the path into the realm of creativity. If study brings knowledge, and imagination spiritual vision, knowledge of the occult script brings magic. It brings direct insight into the laws of nature that slumber in things, direct knowledge of their very essence.

You can find many who make use of occult signs, even people like Eliphas Levi. This can provide an idea of what the signs look like, but not much can be learned, unless one is knowledgeable about them already. What is found in books on the subject is usually erroneous. The signs used to be regarded as sacred, at least by the initiates. If we go back far enough, we find that strict rules concerning their secrecy were imposed, incurring severe punishment if broken, to ensure they were not used for unworthy purposes.

The fourth stage is known as the *preparation of the philosopher's stone* (the stone of the wise). What is written about it is completely misleading; often it is such grotesque nonsense that if true anyone would be entitled to be scornful. What I am going to say will give you a great deal of insight into the truth of the matter.

At the end of the eighteenth century there appeared in an earnest periodical a notice concerning the philosopher's stone. It was clear from the wording of the notice that its author had some knowledge of the matter, yet gave the impression that he did not fully understand. The notice read: The philosopher's stone is something that all are acquainted with, something they often handle, and is found all over the world. It is just that people do not know that it is the philosopher's stone. A peculiar description of what the philosopher's stone was supposed to be, yet word for word quite correct.

Consider for a moment the process of human breathing. The regulation of the breath is connected with the discovery, or preparation of, the philosopher's stone. At present human beings inhale oxygen and exhale carbon dioxide, that is, what is exhaled is a compound of oxygen and carbon. A person inhales oxygen, life-giving air, and exhales carbon dioxide, which is poisonous to both human and animal. If animals, who breathe like human beings, had alone populated the earth, they would have poisoned the air, and neither they nor humans would be able to breathe today. So how does it come about that they are still able to breathe? It is because plants absorb the carbon dioxide, retain the carbon and give back the oxygen for human and animal to use again.

Thus, a beautiful reciprocal process takes place between the breath of humans and animal, and the breath, or rather assimilation, of the plant world. Think of someone who every day earns five shillings and spends two. He creates a surplus, and is in a different position than someone who earns two shillings but spends five. Something similar applies to breathing. However, the significant point is that this exchange takes place between human beings and the vegetable kingdom.

The process of breathing is indeed quite amazing, and we must look at it in a little more detail. Oxygen enters the human body; carbon dioxide is expelled from it. Carbon dioxide consists of oxygen and carbon; the plant retains the carbon and gives a person back the oxygen. Plants that grew millions of years ago are today dug out of the earth as coal. Looking at this coal we see carbon that was once inhaled by the plants. Thus, the ordinary breath, just described, shows how necessary the plant is to a person's life. It also shows that when humans breathe they accomplish only half the process; to complete it they need the plant that possesses something they lack to transform carbon into oxygen.

The Rosicrucians introduce a certain rhythm into the breath, detail of which can only be imparted directly by word of mouth. However, certain aspects can be mentioned without going into details. The pupil receives definite instruction concerning rhythmic breathing accompanied by thoughts of a special nature. The effect must be thought of as comparable to the persistent drip of water that wears away the stone. Certainly even the most highly developed person will not attain, by breathing in the Rosicrucian manner, a complete transformation of the inner life processes from one day to the next. However, the gradual change wrought in the human body leads eventually to a specific goal. At some time in the future a person will be able to transform within his own being carbonic acid into oxygen. Thus, what today the plant does for human beings—transforming the carbonic acid in the carbon—will be done by man himself when the effect of the changed breath has become great enough. This will take place in an organ he will then possess, of which physiology and anatomy as yet know nothing, but which is nevertheless developing. An individual will accomplish the transformation himself. Instead of exhaling carbon a person will use it in his own being; with what he formerly had to give over to the plant he will build up his own body.

All this must be thought of in conjunction with what was said about the Holy Grail: that the purity and chastity of the plant nature would pan over into human nature. When a person's lower nature has reached the highest level of spirituality, it will in that respect be once more at the level of the plant as it is today. The process that takes place in the plant, a person will one day be able to carry out in his own being. He will more and more transform the substance of his present body into the ideal of a plant body, which will be the bearer of a much higher and more spiritual consciousness. Thus, the Rosicrucian pupil learns the alchemy that eventually will enable a person to transform the fluids and substances of the human body into carbon. Thus, what the plant does today—it builds its body from carbon—human beings will one day accomplish. He will build a structure from carbon that will be a person's future body. A great mystery lies hidden in the rhythm of the breath.

You will now understand the notice about the philosopher's stone alluded to earlier. But what is it that human beings will learn in regard to building up the human body in the future? They will learn to create ordinary coal—which is also what diamonds consist of—and from it build their body. Human beings will then possess a higher and more comprehensive consciousness. They will be able to take the carbon out of themselves and use it in their own being. They will form their own substance, that is, plant substance made of carbon. That is the alchemy that builds the philosopher's stone. The human body itself is the retort, transformed in the way indicated.

Thus, behind the rhythm of the breath lies hidden what is alluded to as the search for the philosopher's stone; though what is usually said about it is pure nonsense. The indications given here have only recently reached the public from the School of the Rosicrucians; you will not find them in any books. They represent a small part of the fourth stage: The quest of the philosopher's stone.

The fifth stage, or *knowledge of the microcosm*, the small world, points to something said by Paracelsus to which I have often referred, namely, that if we could draw an extract out of everything around us, it would prove to be like an extract taken from mankind. The substances and forces within us are like a miniature recapitulation of what exists in the rest of nature. When we look at the world around us we can say: What is within us is like a copy of the great archetype that exists outside. For example, take what light has brought about in human beings: It created the eyes. Without eyes we would not see the light; the world would remain dark for us, and likewise for the animals. Those animals that wandered into dark caves to live, in Kentucky, lost the ability to see. If light did not exist we would not have eyes. The light enticed the organs of sight out of the organism. As Goethe said: "The eye is created by the light for the light, the ear by the sound for the sound."

Everything is born from the microcosm. Hence, the secret that under certain instruction and guidance it is possible to enter deeply into the body, and investigate not only what pertains to the body, but to the spiritual realm, and also to the world of nature around us. A person who learns under certain conditions to immerse himself with certain thoughts meditatively in the inner eye will learn the true nature of light. Another area of great significance is between the eyebrows at the root of the nose. By meditatively sinking into this point one learns of important spiritual events that took place as this part of the head was formed from the surrounding world. Thus, one learns the spiritual construction of the human being. He is completely formed and built up by spiritual beings and forces. That is why he can, by delving into his own form, learn about the beings and forces that built up his organism.

A word must be said about delving into one's inner being. This penetrating down from the "I" into the bodily nature, and also the other exercises, ought only to be undertaken after due preparation. Before a start is made the powers of intellect and reason must be strengthened. That is why in Rosicrucian schools the training of thinking is obligatory. Furthermore, the pupil must be inwardly morally strong; this is essential as he may otherwise easily stumble. As a student learns to sink meditatively into every part of his body, other worlds dawn in him.

The deeper aspects of the Old Testament cannot be understood without this sinking into one's inner being. However, it must be done according to certain directions provided by a spiritual scientific training. Everything that is said here in this respect is derived from the spiritual world and can only be fully understood when one is able to discover it again within oneself. Man is born out of the macrocosm; within himself as microcosm he must rediscover its forces and laws. Not through anatomy does man learn about his own being, but through looking into his being and inwardly perceiving that the various areas emit light and sound. The inward-looking soul discovers that each organ has its own color and tone.

Human beings will have direct knowledge of the macrocosm when they learn to recognize, through a Rosicrucian training, what it is in their own being that is created from the universe. Once they know their inner being through meditatively sinking into the eye, or into the point above the root of the nose, human beings can spiritually recognize the laws of the macrocosm. Then, through their own insight, they will understand what it is that an inspired genius describes in the Old Testament. An individual looks into the Akasha Chronicle and is able to follow mankind's evolution through millions of years.

This is insight that can be attained through a Rosicrucian training. However, the training is very different from what is customary. Genuine self-knowledge is neither reached by aimless brooding within oneself nor in believing, as is often taught nowadays, that by looking into oneself the inner god will speak. The power to recognize the great World-Self is attained by immersing oneself in the organs. It is true that down the ages the call has resounded: "Know thyself," but it is equally true that within one's own being the higher self cannot be found. Rather, as Goethe pointed out, one's spirit must widen until it encompasses the world.

That can be attained by those who patiently follow the Rosicrucian path and reach the sixth stage, or *becoming one with the macrocosm.* Immersing oneself in one's inner being is not a path of comfort. Here phrases and generalities do not suffice. It is in concrete reality that one must plunge into every being and phenomenon and lovingly accept it as part of oneself. It is a concrete and intimate knowledge, far removed from merely indulging in phrases like: "Being in harmony with the world"; "being one with the World-Soul," or "melt together with the world." Such phrases are simply valueless compared with a Rosicrucian training. Here the aim is to strengthen and invigorate human soul-forces, rather than chatter about being in tune with the infinite and the like.

When a human being has attained this widening of the self, then, the seventh stage is within reach. Knowledge now becomes feeling; what lives in the soul is transformed into spiritual perception. A person no longer feels that he lives only within himself. He begins to experience himself in all beings: in the stone, plant and animal, in everything into which he is immersed. They reveal to him their essential nature, not in words or concepts, but to his innermost feelings. A time begins when universal sympathy unites him with all beings; he feels with them and participates in their existence. This living within all beings is the seventh stage, or *attaining godliness (Gottseligkeit)*, the blessed repose within all things. When the human being no longer feels confined within his skin, when he feels himself united with all other beings, participating in their existence, and when his being encompasses the whole universe so that he can say to it all: "Thou are that," then the words which Goethe, out of Rosicrucian knowledge, expresses in his poem *The Mysteries* will have meaning: "Who added to the cross the wreath of roses?"

However, these words can be spoken not only from the highest point of view, but from the moment that "the cross wreathed in roses"—what this expresses— has become one's ideal, one's watchword. It stands as the symbol for a human being's overcoming the lower self in which he merely broods, and his rising from it into the higher self that leads a person to the blissful experience of the life and being of all things. He will then understand Goethe's words in the poem: *West-East Divan*

> And until thou truly hast
> This dying and becoming,
> Thou art but a troubled guest
> O'er the dark earth roaming.

Unless one can grasp what is meant by the overcoming of the lower, narrow self and the rising into the higher self, it is not possible to understand the cross as symbol of dying and becoming—the wood representing the withering of the lower self, and the blossoming roses the becoming of the higher self. Nor can the words be understood with which we shall close the subject of Rosicrucianism—words also expressed by Goethe, which as watchword belong above the cross wreathed in roses symbolizing sevenfold man:

The power that holds constrained all humankind,
The victor o'er himself no more can bind.

Von der Gewalt, die alle Wesen bindet
Befreit der Mensch sich, der sich überwindet.

Lecture XII

Richard Wagner and Mysticism

Berlin, March 28, 1907

To link Richard Wagner[1] with mysticism, as we shall do in today's consideration, will easily give rise to objections based on the misconception that to speak about an artist from a particular spiritual-scientific viewpoint is impermissible. Other objections will be directed against mysticism as such.

Today we shall look at Richard Wagner's relation to art on the one hand and mysticism on the other. The objection can be made that Wagner never spoke, or even hinted at, some of the things that will be mentioned. Such an objection is so obvious that anyone would have thought of it before speaking. It must be borne in mind that when a cultural phenomenon such as Richard Wagner is to be considered, one cannot be limited to say only what Wagner spoke about. That would make a discussion on any issue from a higher point of view impossible.

No one would suggest that a botanist or a poet should refrain from expressing what he discovered, or what he felt about plants and other phenomena. When discussing issues, whether cultural or natural, one

169

cannot be limited to say only what the phenomenon conveys. In that case the plant should be able to convey to the botanist the laws of its growth; and the feelings and sentiments it aroused in the poet would be unjustified. The reality is that in the human soul, precisely what the external world is unable to say about itself is revealed.

It is in this sense that what I have to say about the phenomenon that is Richard Wagner must be taken. Certainly a plant knows nothing of the laws, however, it nevertheless grows and develops. Similarly, an artist need not be aware of the laws inherent in his nature of which the observer with spiritual insight is able to speak. The artist lives and creates according to these laws as the plant creates according to laws that are subsequently discovered. Therefore, the objection should not be made that Wagner did not speak about things that will be indicated today.

As regards other objections concerned with mysticism, the fact is that people, educated and uneducated alike, speak of mysticism as of something obscure. In comparison with what is known as the scientific world view, they find it nebulous. This has not always been so. The great mystics of the early Christian centuries, the Gnostics, have thought otherwise, as does anyone with understanding of mysticism. The Gnostics have called it "mathesis," mathematics, not because mysticism is mathematics, but because genuine mystics have striven for a similar clarity in the ideas they derive from spiritual worlds. Properly understood, mysticism, far from being obscure or sentimental, is in its approach to the world crystal clear. Having now shown that the two kinds of objections are invalid, let us proceed with today's considerations.

Richard Wagner can indeed be discussed from the

highest spiritual scientific viewpoint. No seeker after Truth of the nineteenth century strove, his whole life long, more honestly and sincerely to discover answers to the world-riddles than Richard Wagner. His house in Bayreuth he named, "Inner Peace" (*Wahnfried*), saying that there he found peace from his "doubts and delusions" (*sein Wähnen Ruhe fand*). These words already reveal a great deal about Richard Wagner.

What is meant by error and delusion is all too well-known to someone who honestly and sincerely pursues the path to higher knowledge. This happens irrespective of whether the spiritual realm a person believes he will discover finds expression through art, or takes some other form. He is strongly aware of the many deluding images that come to block his path and slow his progress. That person knows that the path to higher knowledge is neither easy nor straightforward—that truth is reached only through inner upheavals and tribulations. Moreover, he is aware that dangers have to be met, but also that experiences of inner bliss will be his. A person who travels the path of knowledge will eventually reach that inner peace that is the result of intimate knowledge of the secrets of the world. Wagner's awareness and experience of these things comes to expression when he says: "I name this house 'Inner Peace' because here I found peace from error and delusions."*

Unlike many artists who attempt to create out of fantasy that lacks substance, Wagner saw from the start an artistic calling as a mission of world historical relevance; he felt that the beauty created by art should also express truth and knowledge. Art was to him

---

"Weil hier mein Wahnen Ruhe fand, Wahnfried sei dieses Haus genannt."

171

something holy; he saw the source of artistic creativity in religious feelings and perceptions. The artist, he felt, has a kind of priestly calling, and that what he, Richard Wagner, offered to mankind should have religious dedication. It should fulfill a religious task and mission in mankind's evolution. He felt that he was one of those who must contribute to their era something based on the fullness of truth and reality.

When spiritual science is properly understood, it will be seen that, far from being a gray theory remote from the real issues, it can help us to understand and to appreciate on his own terms a cultural phenomenon such as Richard Wagner.

Wagner had a basic feeling, an inner awareness, that guided him to the same Truth about mankind's origin and evolution as that indicated by spiritual science. This inner awareness linked him to spiritual science and to all genuine mysticism. He wanted a unification of the arts; he wanted the various branches of art to work together, complementing one another. He felt that the lack, the shortcomings, in contemporary art forms was caused by what he called "their selfishness and egoism." Instead of the various art forms going their separate ways, he saw their working together as an ideal, creating a harmonious whole to which each contributed with selfless devotion. He insisted that art had once existed in such an ideal form. He thought to recognize it in ancient Greece prior to Sophocles,[2] Euripides[3] and others. Before the arts separated, drama and dance, for example, had worked together and had selflessly created combined artistic works. Wagner had a kind of clairvoyant vision of such combined endeavor. Although history does not speak of it, his vision was true and points back to a primordial time when not only the arts but also all spiritual and cultural streams within various people worked together as a harmonious whole.

Spiritual science recognizes that what is known today as art and science are different branches originating from a common root. Whether we go back to the ancient cultures of Greece, Egypt, India or Persia, or to our own Germanic origin, everywhere we find primordial cultures where art and science are not separated. However, this is a past that is beyond the reach of external research, and is accessible only to clairvoyant vision.

In the ancient civilizations, art and science formed a unity that was looked upon as a mystery. Mystery centers existed for the cultivation of wisdom, beauty and religious piety before these became separated and cultivated in different establishments.

We can visualize what took place within the mysteries, with in these temples, which were places of learning and also of artistic performances. We can conjure up before our mind's eye the great dramas, seen by those who had been admitted to the mysteries. As I said, ordinary history can tell us nothing of these things. The performances were dramatic musical interpretations of the wisdom attained within the mysteries, and they were permeated with deep religious devotion. A few words will convey what took place in those times of which nothing is known save what spiritual science has to say. Those admitted to the Mysteries came together to watch a drama depicting the world's creation. Such dramas existed everywhere. They depicted how primordial divine beings descended from spiritual heights and let their essence stream out to become world-substance that they then shaped and formed into the various creature's of the kingdoms of nature: the mineral, plant and animal kingdoms, and that of humans. In other words, divine essence streamed into and formed everything that surrounded us, and it finally celebrated a kind of resurrection within the human soul.

Thoughtful people have always felt that the world is of divine origin, that the divine element attains consciousness in the human soul, and, as it were, looks out through human eyes observing itself in its own creation. This descent and resurrection of the divine element was enacted in Egypt, in the drama of *Osiris*, and dramatized also at various places of initiation in Greece. Those who were permitted to watch saw how art and knowledge combined to depict in dramatic form the creation of the world. Deep feelings of religious piety were called up in the onlooker by this drama, which might be said to be *the* archetypal drama. With reverence and awe the onlooker watched the gods descend into matter, to slumber in all beings, and resurrect within human beings. Filled with awe, the onlooker experienced a mood described once by Goethe in the following significant words: "When man's whole being functions as a healthy entity, and he feels the world to be a great, beautiful, worthy and estimable unity; when pleasure in the harmony gives him pure delight, then, had it self-awareness, the whole universe, feeling it had reached its goal, would shout for joy, and admire the pinnacle of its being and achievement." A wondrous, deeply religious mood filled the hearts of those who watched this drama of the creation of the world.

And not only was a religious mood created, but the drama also conveyed the kind of knowledge that was later imparted in scientific concepts to explain the creation of the world and its beings. However, at that time one received, in the form of pictures, a knowledge that was both scientific and religious. Science and religion were one.

Richard Wagner had a dim feeling that such harmony had once existed. He looked back to a very old culture in ancient Greece that still had a religious character. He saw that in gray antiquity music, drama, dance and architecture did not operate as separate undertakings; they all functioned in conjunction with one another: Knowledge, art and religion were a unity. He concluded that as they separated the arts became self-seeking, egoistical. Wagner looked back as it were to a far distant past when human beings were not so individual, when a person felt as a member of his class, of his whole tribe, when the folk spirit was still regarded as a concrete reality. In that ancient time a natural selflessness had existed. And the thought came to him that man, in order to become an individual, a personality, had to leave the old clan-community to enable the personal element to assert itself. Only in this way could man become a free being, but the price was a certain degree of egoism.

Wagner looked back to what in a primordial past had held people together in communities, a selflessness that had to be left behind so that human beings could become more and more conscious. He had an intuitive presentiment about the future; he felt that once individual freedom and independence had been attained, humans would have to find the way back to fellowship and caring relationships. Selflessness would have to be consciously regained, and loving kindness once more would have to become a prominent factor of life.

For Wagner the present linked itself with the future, for he visualized as a distant ideal the existence of selflessness within the arts. Furthermore, he saw art as playing a significant role in evolution. Human development and that of art appeared to him to go hand in hand; both became egoistical when they ceased to function as a totality. As we see them today, drama, architecture and dance have gone their independent ways. As humanity grew more and more selfish, so did art. Wagner visualized a future when the arts would once more function in united partnership. Because he saw a commune of artists as a future ideal, he was referred to as "the communist."

He aimed to contribute all he could to bring forth harmony among the arts; he saw this as a powerful means of pouring into human hearts the selflessness that must form the basis for a future fraternity. He was a missionary of social selflessness in the sphere of art; he wanted to pour into every soul the impulse of selflessness that brings about harmony among people. Richard Wagner was truly possessed of a deep impulse of a kind that could only arise and be sustained in someone with a deep conviction of the reality of spiritual life. Richard Wagner had that conviction.

Already his work *The Flying Dutchman* bears witness to his belief in the existence of a spiritual world behind the physical. You must bear in mind that I do not for a moment suggest that Wagner himself was conscious of the things I am indicating. His artistic impulse developed according to spiritual laws, as a plant develops according to laws of which it is not conscious, but which are discovered by the botanist.

When a materialist observes his fellowmen, he sees them as physical entities isolated from one another, their separate souls enclosed within their bodies. He consequently believes that all communication between them can only be of an external physical nature. He regards as real only what one person may say or do to another. However, once there is awareness of a spiritual world behind the physical, one is aware also of hidden influences that act from person to person without a physical agent. Hidden influences stream from soul to soul, even when nothing is outwardly expressed. What a person thinks and feels is not without significance or value for the person towards whom the thoughts and feelings are directed. He who thinks materialistically only knows that one can physically reach and assist another person. He has no notion that his inner feelings have significance for others, or that bonds, invisible to physical sight, link soul to soul. A mystic is well aware of these bonds. Richard Wagner was profoundly aware of their existence.

To clarify what is meant by this, let us look at a significant legend from the Middle Ages that to modern humans is just a legend. However, its author, and anyone who recognizes its mystical meaning, is aware that this legend expresses a spiritual reality. The legend, which is part of an epic, tells us about Poor Henry who suffered from a dreadful illness. We are told that only if a pure maiden would sacrifice herself for him could he be cured of his terrible infliction. This indicates that the love, offered by a soul that is pure, can directly influence and do something concretely for another human life.

Such legends depict something of which the materialist has no notion, namely, that purely spiritually one soul can influence another. Is the maiden's sacrifice for Poor Henry ultimately anything else than a physical demonstration of what a large part of mankind believes to be the mystical effect of sacrifice? Is it not an instance of what the Redeemer on the Cross had bestowed on mankind; is it not an instance of that mystical effect that acts from soul to soul? It demonstrates the existence of a spiritual reality behind the physical that can be sensed by man, and led Wagner to the legend of *The Flying Dutchman*— the legend of a man so entangled in material existence that he can find no deliverance from it. The Flying Dutchman is with good reason referred to as the

"Ahasverus of the sea," that is, The Wandering Jew of the sea.

Ashasverus' destiny is caused by the fact that he cannot believe in a Redeemer; he cannot believe that someone can guide mankind onwards to ever greater heights and more perfect stages of evolution. An Ashasverus is someone that has become stuck where he is; human beings must ascend stage by stage if they are to progress. Without striving, he unites himself with matter, with external aspects of life, and becomes stuck in an existence that goes on and on, at the same level. He pours scorn on Him that leads mankind upwards, and remains entangled in matter. What does that mean? Existence keeps repeating itself for someone who is completely immersed in external life. Materialistic and spiritual comprehension differ, because matter repeats itself, whereas spirit ascends. The moment spirit succumbs to matter, it succumbs to repetition.

That happens in the case of *The Flying Dutchman*. Various peoples related this idea to the discoveries of foreign lands; the crossing of oceans and reaching foreign shores was seen as a means of attaining perfection. He who lacked the urge, who did not sense the spirit's call, became stuck in sameness, in what belongs solely to matter. The Flying Dutchman, whose whole disposition is materialistic, is abandoned by the power to evolve, by the power of love, which is the means to ascend to ever greater perfection. He becomes entangled in matter and consequently in the eternal repetition of the same. Those who suffer inability to ascend, who lack the urge to evolve, must come under the influence of a soul that is chaste and pure. Only an innocent maiden's love can redeem the Flying Dutchman.

A certain relationship exists between a soul that is as

yet untouched by material life and one that has become entangled in it. Wagner has an instinctive feeling for this fact, and portrays it with great power in his dramas. Only someone with his mystical sense, and perception of the spirit behind the physical, would have the courage to take on a cultural mission of the magnitude Richard Wagner has assigned to himself. It has enabled him to visualize music and drama in ways no one has thought of before. He has looked back to ancient Greece, to a time when various art forms still played an integral part in performances, when music expressed what the art of drama could not express, and eternal universal laws were expressed through the rhythm of dance.

In older works of art, where dance, rhythm and harmony still collaborated, he recognized something of the musical-dramatic element of the artistic works of antiquity. He acquired a unique sense for harmony, for tonality in music, but insisted that contributions from related arts were essential. Something from them must flow into the music. One such related art was dance, not as it has become, but the dance that once expressed movements in nature and movements of the stars. In ancient times, dance originated from a feeling for laws in nature. Man in his own movements copied those in nature. Rhythm of dance was reflected in the harmony of the music. Other arts, such as poetry, whose vehicle is words, also contributed, and what could not be expressed through words was contributed by related arts. Harmonious collaboration existed among dance, music and poetry. The musical element arose from the cooperation of harmony, rhythm and melody.

This was what mystics and also Richard Wagner felt as the spirit of art in ancient times, when the various arts worked together in brotherly fashion, when melody, rhythm and harmony had not yet attained their later perfection. When they separated, dance became an art form in its own right, and poetry likewise. Consequently, rhythm became a separate experience, and poetry no longer added its contribution to the musical element. No longer was there collaboration between the arts. In tracing the arts up to modern times, Wagner noticed that the egoism in art increased as human beings egoism increased.

Let us now look at attempts made by Wagner to create something harmonious within the artistic one-sidedness he faced. This is the sphere that reveals his greatness as he searched for the true nature of art.

To Richard Wagner, Beethoven[4] and Shakespeare[5] represented artists who one-sidedly cultivated the two arts he particularly wanted to bring together, music and drama. He only had to look at his own inner being to recognize the impossibility of conveying, merely through words, the whole gamut of human feelings, particularly feelings that do not manifest externally through gestures or words. Shakespeare was in his view a one-sided dramatist because dramatic words on their own are incapable of expressing things of deeper import. Only when inner impulses have become external action, have become part of space and time, can they be conveyed through dramatic art. When watching a drama, one must assume the impulses portrayed to be already experiences that are past. What one witnesses is no longer drama taking place within the. person concerned; it has already passed over into what can be physically seen and heard. Whatever deeper feelings and sensations are the basis for what is portrayed on the stage cannot be conveyed by the dramatist.

In music, on the other hand, Wagner regarded the symphonist, the pure instrumentalist, to be the most one-sided, for he conveyed in wonderful tone and scales the inner drama, the whole range of human feelings, but had no means of expressing impulses once they became gestures, or became part of space and time. Thus, Wagner saw music as able to express the inner life, but unable to convey what came to expression outwardly. Dramatic art, on the other hand, when refusing to collaborate with music, only conveyed impulses when they became externalized.

According to Wagner, Shakespeare conveyed one aspect of dramatic art, and Mozart,[6] Haydn[7] and Beethoven another. In Beethoven's *Ninth Symphony* Wagner sensed something that strove to break away from the one-sidedness of this art form, strove to burst the shell and become articulate, strove to permeate the whole world and envelop mankind with love. Wagner saw it as his mission not to let this element remain as it was in the *Ninth Symphony*, but to bring it out still further into space and time. He wanted it not only to be an external expression of a soul's inner drama, but also to flow into words and action. He wanted to present on the stage both aspects of dramatic art: in music, the whole range of inner sensations, and in drama, the aspect of those inner sensations that come to external expression. What he sought was a higher unity of Shakespeare and Beethoven. He wanted the whole of humanity represented on the stage.

When we watch some action taking place on the stage, we should become aware of more than can be perceived by eyes and ears. We should be able to be aware also of deeper impulses residing in the human soul. This aspect caused dissatisfaction in Wagner with the old type of opera. Here the dramatist, the poet and the musician worked separately on a production. The poet wrote his part, the musician then came along and interpreted what was written through music. But the task of music is rather to express what poetry by itself cannot express. Human nature consists of an inner as well as an outer aspect. The inner cannot be portrayed through external means; the outer aspect can indeed be dramatized, but words are incapable of conveying impulses that live within human beings. Music should not be there to illustrate the poetry, but to complete it. What poetry cannot express should be conveyed by music.

That was Wagner's great ideal and the sense in which he wanted to create. He assigned to himself the mission to create a work of art in which music and poetry worked together selflessly. Wagner's basic idea was of mystical origin; he wanted to understand the whole human being, the inner person as well as what he revealed outwardly. Wagner knew that within human beings a higher being resides, a higher self that was only partially revealed in space and time. He sought to understand that higher entity that rises above the everyday. He felt that it must be approached from as many sides as possible. His search for the superhuman aspect of man's being, for that which rises above the merely personal, led him to myths. Mythical figures were not merely human, they were superhuman: They revealed the superhuman aspect of a person's being. Characters like Siegfried and Lohengrin do not display qualities belonging to a single human being, but to many. Wagner turned to the superhuman figures portrayed in myths because he sought understanding of the deeper aspects of the human being.

A clear look at his work reveals how deep an insight he had attained into mankind's evolution. In *The Ring of the Nibelung* and *Parsifal* we witness, powerfully presented, great riddles of humanity's existence. They reveal his intuitive perception, his deep feelings for all mankind.

We can do no more than turn a few spotlights on Wagner's inner experiences as an artist. In so doing we soon discover his strong affinity with what could be called "man's mythical past." His particular interest in the figure of Siegfried can easily be understood when seen in connection with his concept of mankind's evolution. Looking back to ancient times, Wagner saw that formerly the bond between human beings was based on selfless love within the confines of a tribe. Human consciousness at that time was duller; he did not yet experience personal independence. Each one felt himself, not so much an individual, but rather as a member of his tribe. He experienced the tribal soul as a reality.

Wagner felt that especially traits in European culture can be traced back to the time when natural instinctive love united human beings in interrelated groups, a time of which spiritual science also speaks when showing that everything in the world evolves, and that today's clear consciousness gradually evolved from a different type, of which there are still residues. In pictures of dream-consciousness Wagner recognized echoes of a former picture-consciousness that had once been the normal consciousness of all mankind. The waking consciousness of today replaced a much duller type; while it lasted, human beings were much closer to one another. As Wagner recognized, those related were bound together by natural love connected with the blood. Not until later did individuality, and with it egoism, assert itself. However, this constitutes a necessary stage in man's evolution.

The subject I shall now bring up will be familiar to those acquainted with spiritual science, but others may find it somewhat strange. The lucid day-consciousness now existing in Europe evolved from the very different consciousness of a primordial human race that preceded our own—a humanity that existed on Atlantis, a continent situated where the Atlantic Ocean is now. Those who take note of what goes on in the world will be aware that even natural science speaks of an Atlantean continent. A scientific journal, *Kosmos,* recently carried an article about it. Physical conditions on Atlantis were very different; the atmosphere in which the ancestors of today's European lived was a mixture of air and water. Large areas of the continent were covered with huge masses of dense mist. The sun was not seen as we see it, but surrounded by enormous bands of color due to the masses of mist. In Germanic legends a memory is preserved of that ancient country, and given descriptive names such as *Niflheim* or *Nibelungenheim.* As the flood gradually submerged the Atlantean continent, it also gave shape to the German plains. The Rhine was regarded as a remnant of the Atlantean "Being of Mist" that once covered most of the countries. The water of the Rhine was thought to have originated in *Nibelungenheim* or *Nebelheim (Nebel* means "mist"), to have come from the dense mist of ancient Atlantis. Through a dreamlike consciousness, full of premonition, all this is told in sagas and myths wherein is described how conditions caused the people to abandon the area and how, as they wandered eastwards, their dull consciousness grew ever more lucid while egoism increased.

A consequence of the former dull consciousness was a certain selflessness, but with the clearer air, consciousness grew brighter and egoism stronger. The vaporous mist had enveloped the people of Atlantis with an atmosphere saturated with wisdom, selflessness and love. This selfless, love-filled wisdom flowed with the water into the Rhine and reposed beneath it as wisdom, as gold. But this wisdom, if taken hold of by egoism, provides it with power. As they went eastward, the former inhabitants of Atlantis saw the Rhine embracing the hoard of the gold of wisdom that had once been a source of selflessness. All this is intimated in the world of sagas that took hold of Wagner. He had such inner kinship with that lofty spiritual being who preserves memory of the past, whose spirit lives in sagas and myths, that he extracted from myths the whole essence of his view of the world. We therefore witness, dramatized on the stage and echoing through his music, the consequences of human egoism.

We see the Ring closing, as Alberich takes the gold of the Rhine from the *Rhine Maidens*. Alberich is representative of the Nibelungs, who have become egoistic, of the human being that forswears the love through which he is a member of a unity—a clan or tribe. Wagner links to the plan that weaves through the legend the power of possession—that the ancient world arises before his mind's eye, the world that has produced Walhalla, the world of Wotan, and of the ancient gods. They represent a kind of group-soul possessing traits that a people have in common. But when the Ring closes around man's "I," the individual too is taken hold of by greed for gold.

Wagner sensitively portrays what lives in Wotan as group-soul qualities, and in human beings become egoistic craving for the Rhine-gold. We hear it in his music; how could one fail to hear it? It should not be said that something arbitrary is at this point inserted in the music. No human ear could fail to hear in that long E-flat major in the Rhine-gold the impact of the emerging human "I." Wagner's deep mystical sense can be traced in his music.

We are shown that Wotan has to come to terms, not with the consciousness that had become individualized, but with that which had not yet become so, and still strongly acts as group-consciousness. When he tries by stealth to take away the Ring from the giant, he meets this consciousness in the figure of Erda. She is clearly representing the old all-encompassing consciousness through which knowledge is attained clairvoyantly of the whole environment. The words spoken at this point are most significant:

> To thee is known
> What lies hidden in the deep,
> What weaves in air and water
> Through mountain and valley.
> Thou breathest through
> The wele of existence;
> When heads ponder
> Thy sense emerges.
> It is said that to thee
> All things are known.

The old consciousness that held sway in Nebelheim cannot be better described than in the words:

> My sleep is a dreaming
> My dream is a musing
> My musing is ruled by wisdom.

The old consciousness was a dreaming consciousness, but in this dream human beings knew of the whole surrounding world. The dream encompassed the depth of nature and spun its wisdom from person to person, whose musing and actions all stemmed from this dreaming consciousness. Wotan meets it in the figure of Erda with the result that a new consciousness arises.

What is of a higher order is always depicted in myths and sagas as a female figure. In Goethe's *Faust* it is indicated in the words of the *Chorus Mysticus:* "The eternal feminine draws us upwards and on." Various peoples have depicted a person's inner striving towards a higher consciousness as a union with a higher aspect of the being that is seen as feminine. What is depicted as a marriage is a person's union with the cosmic laws that permeate and illumine his soul. For example, in ancient Egypt we see Isis, and as always the female figure that is looked up to as the higher consciousness has characteristics that correspond to those of the particular people. What a people feels to be its real essence, its true nature, is depicted as a female figure corresponding to this ideal—a feminine aspect with which the individual human being becomes united after death, or also while still living.

As we have seen, man can rise above the sensual, either by leaving it behind, and in death uniting with the spirit, or he may attain the union while still living by attaining spiritual sight. In either case, this higher self is depicted in Germanic myths as a female figure. The warrior who fought courageously and died on the battlefield is regarded by ancestors of today's Middle European as someone who, on entering the spiritual world, would be united with this higher aspect of his being. Hence, the Walkyries are shown to approach the dying warriors and carry them up into spiritual realms. Union with the Walkyrie represents union with the higher consciousness. The Walkyrie Brunnhilde is created through the union of Wotan and Erda. Siegfried is to be united with her and guided into spiritual life. Thus, the daughter of Erda represents the higher consciousness of initiation. Siegfried represents the new, the different human being that has come into existence. Because of the configuration and higher perfection of his inner being, he is united with the Walkyrie already in life.

The hidden wisdom in Germanic legends comes to expression in Wagner's artistic creation. He shows that through the *Götterdämmerung* (Twilight of the Gods), the old group-soul consciousness must die out as the new individual consciousness develops in *Siegfried*. Wagner had a deep awareness of the great mysteries connected with mankind's evolution. A human being's inner experiences he expressed through music, his action through dramatic art.

His sense for the mystical aspect of evolution enabled him to portray a person's higher development. It made him place at the centre of one of his dramas the figure of Lohengrin. Who is Lohengrin? He can be understood only when seen on the background of the momentous upheavals taking place all over Europe at the time when the legend was living reality. Only then can we understand what Wagner had in mind when he depicts Lohengrin's relationship with the Lady he names as Elsa von Brabant.Throughout Europe a new epoch was dawning; An individual's striving personality was coming to the fore. Though described in prosaic terms, these phenomena hide events of greatest significance. In France, Scotland, England and as far away as Russia, a new social structure was developing, in the form of the "Tree City." In rural districts, people still lived in groups, in clans; those who wanted to escape flocked to the cities. The urban environment promoted individual consciousness and feelings of independence. People in the city were those who wanted to strip off the bonds of clan or tribe; they wanted to live their own lives in their own way.

In reality a mighty revolution was taking place. Up till then a person's name decided where he belonged and his status. In the city, a person's name was of no importance, family background of no concern. What counted was personal ability; in the city individuality developed. The evolution from selflessness to individuality became an evolution from individuality to brotherhood. The legend depicted this. In the middle of the Middle Ages the old social structure was being replaced with a new structure, within which each person contributed according to his individual capacity.

Formerly, Leaders and rulers, were always descended from priestly and aristocratic families. The fact that they came from such a background was what mattered; they must have the "right" blood. In the future that would be of no account; someone chosen as leader might be completely unknown as regards descent, and it would be regarded as irreverent to link him with a particular name. The ideal was seen in the great individuality, in the anonymous sage who continued to grow and develop; he was not significant because of his descent, but because of what he was. He was a free individual acknowledged by others just because his achievements were his own.

In this sense, Lohengrin comes before us as representative of man, leading men to freedom and independence. The lady who becomes his wife represents the consciousness described as that of city-dweller of the Middle Ages. He who mediates between the Lofty Being that guides mankind and the people is always associated with great individuality, and is always known by a specific name. Through spiritual knowledge he is known by the technical name "Swan," which denotes a particular stage of higher spiritual development. The Swan mediates between ordinary people and the Lofty Being that leads humanity. We see a reflection of this in the legend of Lohengrin.

If we are to do justice to the wisdom found in legends, to things revealed through Wagner's artistry, we must bring to it an open mind and mobile ideas. If taken in a narrow, pedantic sense, we are left with empty words instead of being inwardly fired with enthusiasm by the far-reaching vistas opened up through his work. I must be permitted to bring these things before you in concepts that point to a greater perspective. A figure like Lohengrin must be presented in light of its world-historical background and significance. And we must recognize that an understanding of this significance dawned in Wagner, enabling him to give it artistic form.

The same also applies to Wagner's comprehension of the Holy Grail. We concerned ourselves with the Holy Grail in the previous lecture: "Who are the Rosicrucians?" It is indeed a remarkable fact that at a certain moment there arose in Wagner an inkling of the great teaching that flourished in the Middle Ages. Before that happened, another idea, as it were, prepared the way, but first it led him to create a drama called *The Victor;* this was in 1856.

The Victor was never performed, but the idea it embodied was incorporated into his *Parsifal. The Victor* depicted the following:

Ananda, a youth of the Brahman caste, was loved by a Tschandala maiden; because of the caste system he cannot reciprocate the love. Ananda became a follower of Buddha, and he eventually conquered his human craving: He gained victory over himself. To the maiden was then revealed that in a former life she was a Brahman and had overcome her love for the youth who was then of the Tschandala caste. Thus, she too was a victor. She and Ananda were spiritually united.

Wagner renders a beautiful interpretation of this idea, taking it as far as reincarnation and karma in the Christian-Anthroposophical sense. We are shown that the maiden herself, in a former life, brought about the present events. Wagner has worked on this idea in 1856.

On Good Friday, 1857, he was sitting in the Retreat, "the sanctuary on the green hill." Looking out over the fields watching the plants come to life, sprouting from the earth, an inkling arose in him of the power of the germinating force emerging from the earth in response to the rays of the sun: a driving force, a motivating force that permeates the whole world and lives in all beings; a force that must evolve, that cannot remain as it is; a force that, to reach higher stages, must pass through death. Watching the plants, he felt the force of sprouting life, and turning his gaze across the Lake of Zürich to the village; he contemplated the opposite idea, that of death—the two polar concepts to which Goethe gives such eloquent expression in his poem, *Blessed Longing*.

> And until thou truly hast,
> This dying and becoming,
> Thou are but a troubled guest
> O'er the dark earth roaming.

Goethe rewrote the words in his hymn to nature saying: "Nature invented death to have more life; only through death can she create a higher spiritual life."

On Good Friday, as the symbol of death came before mankind in remembrance, Wagner sensed the connection between life, death and immortality. He felt a connection between the life sprouting from the earth and the Death on the Cross, the Death that is also the source of a Christian belief that life will ultimately be victorious over death, will become eternal life. Wagner sensed an inner connection between the sprouting life of spring and the Good Friday belief in Redemption, the belief that from Death on the Cross springs Eternal Life. This thought is the same as that contained in the Quest for the Holy Grail, where the chaste plant blossom, striving towards the sun, is contrasted with human desire filled nature. On the one hand Wagner recognized that human beings steeped in desires; on the other he looked towards a future ideal—the ideal that human beings shall attain a higher consciousness through overcoming their lower nature, shall attain a higher fructifying power, called forth by the Spirit.

Looking towards the Cross, Wagner saw the blood flowing from the Redeemer, the symbol of Redemption, being caught in the Grail Chalice. This picture, linked itself within him to the life awakening in nature. These thoughts were passing through Wagner's soul on Good Friday, 1857. He jotted down a few words that later became the basis from which he created his magnificent Good Friday drama. He wrote: "The blossoming plant springs from death; eternal life springs from the Death of Christ." At that moment Wagner had an inner awareness of the Spirit behind all things, of the Spirit victorious over death.

For a time other creative ideas pushed those concerned with *Parsifal* into the background. They came to the fore once more near the end of his life, when, clearer than before, they conveyed to him a person's path of knowledge. Wagner portrayed the path to the Holy Grail to show the cleansing of a human beings' desire nature. As an ideal this is depicted as a pure holy chalice whose image is the plant calyx's chaste fructification to new creation by the sunbeam, the holy lance of love. The sunbeam enters matter as Amfortas' lance enters sinful blood. But there the result is suffering and death. The path to the Holy Grail is portrayed as a cleansing of the sinful blood of lower desires till, on a higher level, it is as pure and chaste as is the plant calyx in relation to the sunbeam. Only he who is pure in heart, unworldly, untouched by temptation, so that he approaches the Holy Grail as an "innocent fool" filled with questions of its secret, can discover the path.

Wagner's *Parsifal* is born out of his mystical feeling for the Holy Grail. At one time he meant to incorporate the idea into his work *Die Wibelungen,* an historical account of the Middle Ages. He wanted to elevate the concept of Emperor by letting Barbarossa journey to the East in search of the original spirit of Christianity, thus combining the Parsifal legend with history of the Middle Ages. This idea led to his wonderful artistic interpretation of the Good Friday tradition, so that it can truly be said that Wagner has succeeded in bringing religion into art, in making art religious.

In his artistic new creation of the Good Friday tradition, Wagner had the ingenious idea of combining the subject of faith with that of the Holy Grail. On the one hand stands the belief that mankind will be redeemed, and on the other, that through perfecting its nature humanity itself strives towards redemption; the belief that the Spirit permeating mankind—a drop of which lives in each individual as his higher self—in Christ Jesus foreshadowed humanity's redemption. All this arose as an inner picture in Wagner's mind already on that Good Friday in 1857 when he recognized the connection between the legend of Parsifal and Redemption through Christ Jesus.

We can begin to sense the presence of the Christ within mankind's spiritual environment when, with sensitivity and understanding, we absorb the story of the Holy Grail. And it can deepen to concrete inner spiritual experience when we sense the transition from the midnight of Maundy Thursday—events of Maundy Thursday—to those of Good Friday, which symbolize the victory of nature's resurrection.

Wagner's *Parsifal* was inspired by the festival of Easter. He wanted new life to pour into the Christian festivals, which originally were established out of a deep understanding of nature. This can be seen especially in the case of the Easter festival, which was established when it was still known that the constellation of sun and moon affected human beings. Today people want Easter celebrated on an arbitrarily chosen date, which shows that the festival is no longer experienced as it was when there was still a feeling for the working of nature. When the spirit was regarded as a reality it was sensed in all things. If we could still sense what was bequeathed to us through traditions in regard to the festivals, then we would also have a feeling for how to celebrate Good Friday. Richard Wagner did have that feeling, just as he also perceived that the words of the Redeemer: "I am with you to the end of the world," called human beings to follow the trail that led to the lofty ideal of the Holy Grail. Then people who lived the Truth would become redeemers.

Mankind is redeemed by the Redeemer. But Wagner adds the question: "When is the Redeemer redeemed?" He is redeemed when He abides in every human heart. As He has descended into the human heart, the human heart must ascend. Something of this was also felt by Wagner, for from the motif of faith he lets sound forth what is the mystical feeling of mankind in these beautiful words from *Parsifal:*

Greatest Healing Wonder:

Redemption for the Redeemer!

These words truly show Wagner's deep commitment to the highest ideal a person can set himself: to approach that Spiritual Power that came down to us and lives in our world. When we are worthy, we bring what resounds at the close of Richard Wagner's *Parsifal:* Redemption for the Redeemer.

Lecture XIII

The Bible and Wisdom

Berlin, April 26, 1907

In a previous lecture,* we discussed spiritual science in relation to religious records. Today we shall attempt to enter more deeply into the Bible, at least in a few instances. The Bible is after all a religious document that today is known to every educated person. From the spiritual scientific point of view, it will be easiest if, in our approach, we start with the New Testament. In the earlier lecture, we discussed how certain critical comments concerning the Bible are to be understood in the light of spiritual science, in particular those concerned with the actual writing of the four Gospels and Scriptures in the Old Testament. Today we shall look at more positive aspects and, while bearing in mind what was dealt with in the previous lecture, go straight to the subject from the spiritual scientific viewpoint.

You will be aware that someone who, out of a heartfelt need of his Christian faith, turns to the four Gospels known as the Gospel according to Matthew, to Mark, to Luke and to John, comes up against what appear to

---

*This lecture was not recorded.

be insoluble contradictions. A modern person, however great his faith, can have no notion of how differently one approached the Bible in an earlier more religious age. Nor can a person have any idea of the significance attached to the word Bible or to the expression, the Word of God. We must realize that for centuries the faithful were in no doubt that the writers of the religious records were inspired. Consequently, every word in the Bible was regarded as holy, as from divine inspiration only truth could come. People saw the Bible as dealing with great world questions, and they fastened onto every word, for it was impossible for them to believe that fault could be found in what men of God had written under divine inspiration.

Modern human beings find it difficult to transport themselves into such a mood and attitude. They read the Gospel of Matthew and that of Luke and find two different genealogies of Jesus of Nazareth. Already in the third place, above the name of Joseph, they find in Matthew the name Solomon, in Luke the name Nathan; going further they find many more names that differ, and ask, How is it possible that a document, which for centuries has been considered a source of Truth, can contain such contradictions?

Here we see the seed of all the doubts aroused by disparities in the Gospels and consequently doubt that they were in fact inspired. By subjecting the Gospels to detailed scrutiny we believe to have discovered what can be accepted as more or less genuine. In regard to the fourth Gospel, the conclusion is drawn that as it is so different from the others it cannot be a historical record at all. It is understandable that the modern person becomes critical when faced with contradictions that are impossible to explain away by even the most open-minded individual.

However, we must ask ourselves how it came about that no one for centuries, for millennia, noticed these contradictions that are now criticized. It is difficult to believe that only very stupid people ever handled the Bible. Perhaps it could be argued that only very few people had access to the Bible; before the art of printing, the majority of the faithful did not. Consequently, they could not pass judgment on something about which they were not informed by the leading few who did have access to the Bible. But are we really to believe that those few were all so stupid that they did not notice what is pointed out by today's critics?

Some historians maintain that only slowly, through the power of the church, did these documents come to be appreciated. Reverence for the Bible arose only gradually. It is said that the Bible cannot stand up to close historical investigation. Looking at events that took place in the early Christian centuries, the conclusion is drawn that the Ecumenical Council of Nicea[1] (A.D. 325) decided which Gospels were true, and there it was ordained: "These are the true Holy Scripts." Unprejudiced investigation does not bear this out. Looking back we come to personalities who lived in the early days of Christendom. From them we learn that, for example, in the year A.D. 160 a so-called harmonizing of the Gospels took place. This meant collating the Gospels and bringing them to present a uniform picture, a procedure that was later repeated. And indeed, careful examination of the Gospels as they were in the second century showed that already then they contained what we know as the New Testament. We find that the early Church Fathers in particular spoke with the deepest reverence about the Bible, which suggests that they certainly had the belief that the Bible had been inspired by a higher spiritual source. Already in Origen[2] we encounter the same reverent approach to the biblical records as is later to be found in the faithful, whether of learned or of simple faith.

When these things are considered, all prejudice must be set aside. In the early centuries the attitude of learned people towards Christianity was by no means the same as that of modern people. Today one risks being accused of repudiating the true words of the Bible, of being an agnostic and unfit to call himself a Christian by people with orthodox viewpoints. These people should recognize that to interpret the Bible in ways that differ from their own is not qhe equivalent of doubting its truth. It was the Church Father Augustine[3] who said: "What is known today as Christian religion is ancient; in fact, what was the true primordial religion is today called Christianity."

These words are in great contrast to the usual experience of those who interpret the Bible in the light of spiritual science. The hostility, often coming from family and friends, is nothing short of tragic. Spiritual scientific explanations are harshly rejected as having nothing to do with the Bible. Such reactions are based on complete ignorance of the Bible itself. It is also pretentious, for it proclaims an understanding of the Bible that cannot be faulted. If only such people would recognize that their attitude to the spiritual scientific explanations is in effect like saying: "What I find in the Bible is the only truth."

Spiritual science, far from having a negative approach to the Bible, seeks to unravel its deep truths. The main concern is that these religious records should be properly understood. Those who simply find it more comfortable to remain within views to which they have become accustomed are not in a position to oppose spiritual science. Rejection of true explanations is often based on deep seated hostility, though sometimes it is simply too much effort to learn something new.

No Christian with any understanding of a certain passage from the Sermon on the Mount, often quoted by me, could maintain that attitude. The passage, when rightly translated reads: "Blessed are those who are beggars of the spirit, for within themselves they shall find the Kingdom of Heaven." No words could better or more beautifully express the inner feeling and disposition of the spiritual scientist than this passage from the Sermon on the Mount.

What do we mean by the inner disposition of the spiritual scientist? We mean an inner impulse to strive to develop the deepest kernel of our being, our spirituality. What builds our body comes from substances that surround us; likewise our inner being comes from the spirit that lives, and always did live all about us. Just as it is true that our body is, as it were, a drop from the sea of material reality, so is it true that our soul, our spirit, is a drop from the sea of the all-encompassing Universal Spirit. As the drop of water is of the same substance as the sea from which it is taken, so is that which lives in the deepest recess of the human soul godlike. Human beings are able to recognize God because God lives within them and human beings are themselves spiritual. Furthermore, if a person truly will, he can attain that spiritual world that is all about him. However, for that to come about something is needed—something which can be simply expressed by saying: Do not ever stand still. Human beings must *experience* progress, must be conscious of evolving, rather than merely having faith that it will happen. It means never to lose sight of the fact that not only have human beings developed to their present stage from inferior levels, but also that at every moment they can develop further.

In this instance we are not concerned with the fact that a person's external being has altered in the course of evolution, but rather with the fact that the human soul can climb upwards from stage to stage. In striving for perfection, a human being's soul is capable of improving from day to day. Today we may learn something new; we inwardly grasp something we did not know before; through our will we become capable of achieving something we could not manage before. If we remain at what we understand today, at what our will is capable of today, then we do not evolve. We must never lose sight of the fact that as well as the forces that are already developed within us, we possess others still slumbering. It is comparable to the seeds of new plants that slumber within the seed that has already become a plant. If we never forget that we possess such forces, our will grows stronger; it reaches higher stages of development and we become aware that our soul begins to evolve spiritual eyes and ears. We must not think of this as something trivial, but recognize that the development of the human soul and spirit is of universal significance.

When we see in the physical world, a relationship between animal forms and the noble human form, it does not justify the assumption that a person has developed from the animal, even if natural science has established that, as regards the physical structure, there is greater similarity between the lowest developed human being and the highest developed ape, than between the lowest and highest developed ape. This observation, however, led natural science to regard human beings as having descended from the ape. The famous natural scientist Thomas Henry Huxley[4] spoke about it as a great heresy in 1859. This view influenced practically everything he wrote. However, those who recognize spiritual development say: Granted that man, in regard to his external bodily form, is closer to the highest evolved ape, than the latter to the lowest of its own species, it is equally true that a human being who has reached a certain stage in spiritual development is further from the lowest developed human being, than the latter from the highest evolved animal.

When evolution is followed through, the higher stages are seen to continue up into spiritual realms where what is described by spiritual science takes place, and which to spiritual sight is as much a reality as physical evolution is to physical sight. Spiritual knowledge has always existed. Natural science today only acknowledges an evolution that starts with the lowest animal form and continues up to that of man. Spiritual science is in full agreement with that evolution. It also acknowledges the enormous difference between the lowest form of life, barely visible even through the microscope, and the perfect structure of the human organism. A person's physical structure does indeed pass through innumerable evolutionary stages from the most imperfect to the most perfect.

However, the spiritual scientist sees the evolution of soul and spirit as just as real. The difference he sees is just as great between the highly advanced human being, the initiate, and the person who has barely begun to develop his slumbering forces. An initiate is someone who has attained spiritual faculties by developing to ever greater perfection forces that are inherent in every human soul. The difference between the lower stages of soul development and those attained by an initiate is actually greater than the difference between the lowest living structure and that of human beings. A person who knows that initiates exist also knows that the possibility to develop spiritually is a reality.

With this insight there dawns in the human soul a feeling, an attitude that says: I look up to a godlike ideal of man, the seed of which slumbers within me. I know that in the future it will become reality, though as yet it is only slightly indicated. I know also that I must exert all my powers to attain that ideal. With this insight into spiritual development man becomes a "beggar of the spirit"; he feels himself blessed. In the spiritual scientific sense the passage from the Sermon on the Mount is a truly wonderful saying: "Blessed are those who are beggars of the spirit, for within themselves they shall find the Kingdom of Heaven."

Those acquainted with old linguistic usage will not imagine that what is here meant by heaven is something existing in an unknown beyond. In those days heaven was understood to be wherever man is. Where we are is where heaven is, that is, the spiritual world. A blind person will see the world full of color when successfully operated upon; likewise a person whose spiritual eyes are opened sees around him a new world. What a person sees was actually always about him, but he sees it in a new way. He sees the way he must be able to see if he is to attain his higher humanity. He will know that heaven is not somewhere else, is not in another place or time. He recognizes the Truth when Christ says: "Heaven is in the midst of you."

Where we are is the Kingdom of Heaven; it penetrates everything physical. As ice swims in water out of which it has condensed, so does matter swim in a sea of spirit out of which it has condensed. Everything physical is condensed, transformed spirit.

In the animal kingdom we see the physically imperfect side by side with the physically more perfect; in the human kingdom we see all stages of spiritual development: One person has forged ahead, another remained at a lower stage. This indicates how in the spiritual scientific sense, human beings are connected with evolution. One person's interest lies in the realm of modern science, another's in the realm of human cultural development from the savage to the highly advanced individual who has attained insight into the spiritual world around him. The initiates always had insight into all the stages of human spiritual development. One spoke of the initiate as of someone who possessed greater knowledge than anyone else. Such initiates were mentioned in every epoch. Let us make it clear in what sense one spoke of those initiated into the spiritual world.

We have often discussed the fact that in ancient times people had clairvoyant consciousness. The term "clairvoyant" did not refer to clarity, but to the fact that it penetrated through the external to the soul. A residue of this dull, dim consciousness can be seen in today's consciousness in dreams. Our clear waking consciousness developed from it. At the time when in general a person's consciousness was dull and dim, though clairvoyant, a few were initiates. In what sense did this consciousness differ from that of the rest of humanity? It differed because those who were initiates already experienced something of the type of consciousness that mankind in general attained today. They reached at an earlier stage something that belonged to the future. Already they saw the world the way humanity in general sees it today. That is to say, they investigated the world through the physical organs, through sight and hearing, and grasped things through the intellect. That is the sense in which they were initiates. An initiate attained ahead of time something that belonged to the future. There are also initiates today; who have already developed the higher clairvoyant consciousness, that is, the higher perception that mankind in general will possess in the future. The initiate was looked up to in ancient times by those who understood. They said to themselves: The initiate's outlook, his understanding of the world, is the outlook and understanding all human beings will possess in the future. He is the embodiment of a future ideal; through what he is, is revealed what we shall become. In the course of time the initiate will lead a great number of human beings to attain what he has attained.

In this sense, the initiate was a prophet or a messiah. He was also called a "first-born." But those to be initiated had to pass through many stages. Before the stage of initiation was attained, many different degrees of learning and schooling of the will must be passed through. As a plant must go through many stages from root through leaf and blossom before bearing fruit, so a human being strove upwards in stages of ever greater insight, till finally the pupil became an initiate. He attained progress by going through certain schooling that anyone can adopt. Those who deny that such a schooling is possible do so out of ignorance. They have as yet not discovered that through schooling, a person's spiritual eyes and ears can be opened so that he attains a higher kind of perception. It is the task of spiritual science to provide knowledge of such schooling. In my book *Knowledge of the Higher Worlds and its Attainment*, you will find this subject is dealt with in great detail. There are many reasons why this knowledge is essential in our time. I will mention just one.

It is a tragedy that because human intellect and reasoning power have progressed too far, he is no longer able to believe in the ancient religious records. He no longer experiences them as the embodiment of the words of God. The fact that the human soul no longer receives the ancient knowledge causes it torment and depression. What is needed is the knowledge presented in a new form, and this is what spiritual science wishes to provide. Those who are initiates today are able—as were initiates in ancient times—to foresee humanity's future evolution. However, human development must follow certain rules. Just as one must adopt a definite method if one wishes to become an astronomer, likewise must a certain method be adopted if one is to develop spiritually. No one should wish to attempt to do so without guidance; that would be like wishing to become a mathematician without consulting any authority. Someone needs show the way, but no other kind of authority is required, and it is nonsense to talk about blind faith and dependence in relation to spiritual science.

Throughout the millennia, right back to antiquity, there were always books in existence, or rather not actual books, but traditions handed down by word of mouth, of the rules of initiation. These rules were not permitted to be written down. They consisted of indications that the candidate for initiation had to follow when setting out to attain all the stages of development that lead to initiation. Even today certain indications are not written down, but imparted directly to those worthy to receive them. These indications the neophyte must observe if he is to attain the highest goal. A principle of initiation was always in existence, that is rules for the birth of the spirit in man. He who dedicated himself to spiritual striving was guided through exercises and conduct of life on ever higher levels. Once the highest was attained, the initiate would reveal to him the deepest secrets.

One word more about this codex for initiation. Today things are different; the procedure of initiation also progresses. In ancient times, the neophyte was brought to a condition of ecstasy. This word had a different meaning; it did not indicate "being out of one's mind" but becoming conscious on a higher level. The spiritual guide led the neophyte to this condition of higher consciousness. Strict rules were observed; the prescribed length for the condition to last was three and one-half days. This procedure is no longer followed; today the consciousness is not subdued. But in ancient times a state of ecstasy, of rapture, was produced during which the neophyte knew nothing of what went on about him; to the external world he was like someone asleep. However, what was experienced in this condition differed considerably from the experiences of a contemporary person when the external objects disappear from his consciousness, on falling asleep. The neophyte experienced a world of spirit; all about him there was light, astral light. This is different from physical light; it appears like a sea of spirituality out of which spiritual beings emerge. If a very high stage had been attained, sound would also be experienced. What in the ancient Pythagorean schools was called "the harmony of the spheres" was heard. (What today we understand intellectually as universal laws are experienced as a kind of spiritual music at this level of consciousness. Spiritual forces are revealed as harmony and rhythm, but must not be thought of as ordinary music. The spiritual world, the heavenly world, resounds in the astral light.) In this world into which the neophyte was led, he learned to know stages of godliness that humanity will attain in a far distant future. During the three and one-half days a person experienced all this as reality, as Truth.

These things may sound extraordinary to many, but there are, and always were people who recognize that a spiritual reality exists that is as real as the one perceived through physical senses. After three and one-half days the initiate was guided back to the sense world enriched with knowledge of spiritual existence, and prepared to bear witness of the spiritual world. All initiates on their return to the ordinary world uttered certain words that were always the same: "Oh my God, how thou has glorified me!" These words expressed the sensation felt by the one just initiated as he set foot again in the everyday world. Those who guided the initiation knew all the stages by heart; later when writing came more into use certain things were written down. But there always existed a typical or standard description of the life of an initiate. One said as it were: "He who is accepted into the cult to be initiated must live according to certain rules and pass through the experience which culminates with the words: "Oh my God, how thou hast glorified me!"

If you could depict the way an initiate necessarily had to live, the way you could depict someone wishing to carry out experiments in a chemical laboratory, then you would obtain a picture typical of someone striving to attain a higher development, typical of someone to be awakened to a higher life. Such a codex of initiation always existed or was at least known by heart by those concerned with initiation. Knowing this, we can understand why the descriptions of different initiates of various people are similar. This fact contains a great secret, a great mystery. The people always looked up to their initiates, insofar as they knew of them. What was said about initiates was not the kind of thing modern biographers relate about famous people; what was told was the course of the spiritual life experienced by the initiate. We can therefore understand why descriptions of the life of Hermes,[40] Zarathustra,[41]

Buddha,[42] Moses[43] and Christ are similar. It was because they had to experience a certain life if they were to become initiates. Their lives were typical of that of an initiate.

In the outer structure of the spiritual biography we can always see a picture of the initiate. We can now answer the question: Who were the writers of the gospels? In my book, *Christianity as Mystical Fact*, you will find this question answered in greater detail from the viewpoint of spiritual science, and also indications of the spiritual authenticity of the Gospels. Here I can only give a few hints! In my book is explained that what is written in the Gospels is derived from ancient records of initiation. Naturally what initiates wrote differs in regard to incidentals, but all essentials were always the same. We must realize that the writers of the Gospels had no other sources than the ancient codex of initiation. When we look into the details, we recognize in the Gospels different forms of initiation. They differ because the writers knew initiation from different regions. This we shall understand when we consider how the writers of the Gospels were connected with Christ.

The best way to form an idea of this connection is to think of the significant words at the beginning of the Apocalypse.[5] The One who dictates the content to John is named "The First and the Last, the Alpha and Omega." This refers to that Being who is always present, through all changes from generation to generation, from human race to human race, from planet to planet; the Being that endures through all transformations. If we call this Being God, of whom a particle lives within each of us, then we sense our relationship to this Alpha and Omega. Indeed, we recognize it as the ultimate ideal, the ultimate goal of striving human beings.

At this point we must remind ourselves of a forgotten custom. Nowadays, names are bestowed more or less haphazardly. We do not feel any real connection between a person and his name. The further back we go in human history, the greater the importance and significance of the name. Certain rules were observed when a name was given. Even not so very long ago, it was the custom to consult the calendar, and give the newly born the name mentioned on the day of its birth. It was assumed that the child had sought to be born on the day that bore that name. When someone attained initiation he was given a new name, an initiation name that expressed a person's innermost nature, expressed what the spiritual leader had recognized to be his significance to the world.

As you know, we find in the New Testament many sayings attributed to Jesus. Their deeper meaning can be understood only if approached from the viewpoint of initiation and understanding of the significance of bestowing names. For example, if someone had reached an as yet not so high level spiritually, and one wished to give him a corresponding name, it would be one that expressed characteristics of the astral body. If a person had reached a higher level, the name would express characteristics of the ether body. If it was to express something that was typical, it would be derived from characteristics of the physical body. In ancient times, names were related to the person and expressed his essential nature. You will remember that in the Gospels Jesus often describes what He is in words that refer back to the word "I." This you find particularly in the Gospel according to John.

We must now bear in mind that we distinguish four members in a person's being: physical body, ether body, astral body and "I." The "I" will increase more and more. It is inherent in a person's "I" to develop towards initiation. In undeveloped people it is imperfect, in the initiate perfect and powerful. You will now understand from the way names were given that Christ did not refer to Himself as an ordinary human being with an ordinary human "I." In John's Gospel He often indicates that He is identical with the "I am," as in the sentence, "I and the Father are One." He describes Himself as identical with the human being's deepest nature. This He does because He is the Eternal, the Christ, the Alpha and Omega.

Those who lived at the time of Christ saw Him as a Divine Being who carried about Him a physical body, a being in whom the spirit is the all-important, whereas in human beings the physical is the all-important. For human beings the outstanding characteristic was expressed in the name. When we ponder this we find that it opens the door to many of the mysteries contained in the Bible. We shall understand what it means when Moses stands before Jehovah as messenger and asks: "Whom shall I tell the people has sent me?" And we hear the significant words: "Tell the people that the 'I am' sent thee." What does Jehovah refer to? He points to the deepest and most significant aspect of a person's being, to that which lies deeply hidden in every human soul, to the human's "I." We find that when we come to this fourth member, then the "I" is a name we must bestow on ourselves. The godlike within human beings must speak. It begins to speak in what appears to live in human beings as a mere point , aa a tiny insignificant seed, which can however develop to infinite greatness. It is this aspect of a person's being that gave Moses his task and said: "Tell them that the 'I am' sent thee." A divine seed lies within every human soul enveloped in the physical, etheric and astral bodies. It appears as a mere point to which we say: "I am." But this member of our being, which appears so insignificant, will become by far the most important. The essence of the human being tells Moses: "I am the I am."

This illustrates the significance connected with the giving of a name. Whenever a reference is made to the "I am" it is also a reference to a certain moment in humanity's evolution that is indicated in the Bible, and often referred to in my lectures: the moment when physical man became an ensouled being. Physical man, as he is today, has developed from lower stages. Only when the Godhead had endowed him with a soul was man able to develop higher stages of his being. What descended from the bosom of the Godhead sank into the physical body and developed it further. In the Bible this moment is indicated in only a few words; it actually stretched over long epochs. Before that time, the human bodies did not possess what is essential—essential also for physical man today—if the "I" is to develop: the ability to breathe through lungs. A human being's physical ancestors did not originally breathe through lungs, which only developed in the course of time from a bladder-like organ. The human being could receive a soul only when he had learned to breathe through lungs. If this whole event is summed up in one sentence, you have the saying in the Bible: "And the Lord God breathed into his nostrils the breath of life, and man became a living soul." In regard to the name Jehovah, we find that it means something like blowing, or rushing wind. The word Jahve expresses the inrush of breath with which the spirit, the "I" drew into man. The physical breath enabled man to receive his soul.

Therefore, in the name Jahve is expressed the nature of the inrushing breath with which the "I am the I am" poured part of its Being into human beings. What we are told in the Bible truly represents a world event depicting the entry into a human being of the eternal aspect of his nature. Whether we think of man as he is today or as he was thousands of years ago, the nature, the "Being of the I" *(Ichwesen)* always was. Think of the highest revelation of this "Eternal I," when all external aspects are irrelevant. Think of a human being in whom can be recognized the most inward nature of the "Eternal I" in all its greatness and might, and you have an idea how the first followers of Christ saw Him. What in ancient time was revealed on earth only as a spark, was revealed in Jesus of Nazareth in its highest glory. He was the greatest initiate because He was the most Godly, so that He could say: "Before Abraham was, I was." He incorporated that which existed before Abraham,[44] Isaac[45] and Jacob.[46] He is that to which striving mankind looks up as the greatest ideal. They are those mentioned in the Sermon on the Mount as: "Blessed are those who are beggars of the spirit, for within themselves they shall find the Kingdom of Heaven." These words applied to the followers of Christ. But how could they give a description of the life of the highest God incarnated? What description would be worthy of Him? Only the one that was contained in the canon of initiation, describing the rules of initiation. There was described the way the one to be initiated must from stage to stage pass through certain experiences which culminated in the words: "Oh my God, how thou hast glorified me!" *(The transcript of this lecture ends at this point.)*

Notes

Lecture I

1. Helena Petrowna Blavatsky (1831-1891) was the founder of the Theosophical Society and a Russian occultist.
2. Ledebur (?) was a chemist from Breslau.
3. Theodor Lipps (1851-1914) was a philosopher.
4. Helen Adams Keller (1880-1968) was an author and lecturer. She was born deaf, blind and mute. She became famous for her triumph over her disabilities.
5. Anne Sullivan (1866-1936) was Helen Keller's teacher. She was partially blind herself.

Lecture II

1. Johann Wolfgang von Goethe (1749-1832) was a German poet, novelist, and playwright.
2. Jacob Minor (1855-1912) was professor of philology.
3. Ernst Haeckel (1834-1919) was a German biologist who supported Darwin's theory of evolution and his theory of ontogeny or the development of an individual organism.
4. Georg Christoph Lichtenberg (1744-1799) was a physicist and satirical writer.
5. Jean Paul (Jean Paul Friedrich Richter, 1763–1825), German author.
6. Georges Léopold Chrétien Couvier (1769-1832) was a French comparative anatomist and the founder of paleontology.

Lecture III

1. Silenus was a drunken attendant of Bacchus and one of the satyrs. He was a personage in Greek mythology.

2. Dionysus was the god of wine and fertility.

3. Friedrich Nietzsche (1844-1900) was a German philosopher, classical scholar and critic of Christianity.

4. Aeschylus (c. 525-456 B.C.) was a dramatist and tragic poet. He is regarded as the "father of tragedy."

5. Arthur Schopenhauer (1788-1860) was a German philosopher.

6. Eduard von Hartmann (1842-1906) was a German philosopher and poet.

Lecture V

1. Friedrich von Schiller (1759-1805), a leading figure in German literature, was a playwright, poet and essayist.

2. Francis of Assisi, Saint (c. 1181-1226) was an Italian Roman Catholic mystic and founder of the Franciscan Order of Monks.

3. Paracelsus (1493-1541) was a Swiss alchemist and physician.

Lecture VI

1. Aristotle (384-322 B.C.) was a Greek philosopher and one of the most influential thinkers of his time.

Lecture VII

1. Friedrich August Wolf (1759-1824) was a philologist.

2. Homer (8th century B.C.) was a Greek epic poet who wrote the *Iliad* and *Odyssey*.

3. Alexander the Great (356-323 B.C.) was King of Macedonia and conqueror of the Persian Empire.

4. Atlantis is a mythical continent, said to have sunk into the sea. Plato describes it in *Timaeus* and *Critias*, and Steiner mentions it frequently.

5. Buddha, Gautama (c. 563-483 B.C.) the founder of Buddhism.

6. Plato (c. 427-347 B.C.) was a Greek philosopher who founded the academy where Aristotle studied.

7. Pythagoras (c. 570-c. 500 B.C.) was a Greek philosopher who founded the Pythagorean school.

8. Hermes was a Greek god and messenger of the gods. He was the god of roads, commerce, invention, cunning, and theft. Identified by the Romans with Mercury.

9. Moses (c. 13th century B.C.) was a Hebrew lawgiver and

prophet who led the Israelites out of Egypt.

10. Zarathustra (c. 6th century B.C.) was a Persian. The religion Zoroastrianism is based on his teachings.

Lecture VIII

1. Friedrich Hölderlin (1770-1843) was among the greatest of German lyric poets. His images were usually derived from classical Greek themes.

2. Moritz Benedict (1835-1920) was a criminologist.

Lecture IX

1. Essenes (200 B.C. to A.D. 100) were a sect that flourished in Palestine. In their monastic community, they strictly observed the law of Moses.

Lecture XI

1. Christian Rosenkreuz (15th century) was the founder of Rosicrucianism, a group of secret brotherhoods claiming esoteric wisdom in the late Middle Ages.

2. Valentin Andreae (1586-1654) theologian, wrote about Rosicrucianism.

3. Charles Robert Darwin (1809-1882) the English naturalist who first formulated the theory of evolution.

4. Holy Grail, a cup or chalice, associated in medieval legend with unusual powers, especially the regeneration of life and water, and later with Christian purity. Became identified with the cup used at the Last Supper and given to Joseph of Arimathea.

Lecture XII

1. Richard Wagner (1813-1883) was a major German opera composer.

2. Sophocles (c. 495 B.C.–406 B.C.) was a great Athenian dramatist and one of the founders of Greek tragedy.

3. Euripides (c. 480 B.C.–406 B.C.), a Greek dramatist.

4. Ludwig van Beethoven (1770-1827) was a German composer born in Bonn.

5. William Shakespeare (1564-1616) was an English poet,

playwright and actor-manager of the Globe Theatre.

6. Wolfgang Amadeus Mozart (1756-1791), Austrian composer.

7. Franz Joseph Haydn (1732-1809), Austrian composer who established the accepted classical forms of the symphony, string quartet, and piano sonata.

Lecture XIII

1. Council of Nicaea was called by Emperor Constantine. It formulated the Nicene Creed in A.D. 325.

2. Origen (c. 185–A.D. 254) was an early Christian Church Father and writer.

3. Augustine, Saint (354-430) a Christian theologian and writer. The most prominent of the Latin Fathers of the Church.

4. Thomas Henry Huxley (1825-1895). He supported Darwin's theory of evolution. He coined the word "agnostic." He also was a natural scientist.

5. Apocalypse was a prophetic revelation about Armageddon. Jewish and Christian writings appeared in Palestine between 200 B.C. and A.D. 1500.

6. Abraham, the biblical father of the Hebrew people and first of the patriarchs, was regarded as the founder of the ancient Hebrew nation.

7. Isaac, the son of Abraham and Sarah.

8. Jacob of the Old Testament was the son of Isaac and Rebecca and was the father of the twelve patriarchs.